The
Kumquat
Statement

The Kumquat Statement

by
JOHN R. COYNE, JR.

COWLES BOOK COMPANY, INC.
NEW YORK

For Pat

INTRODUCTION

by
William F. Buckley, Jr.

It is frequently asked by those who wonder about the silent majority in the student world why so little is heard from those whom under the press of present circumstances one would expect to be moved to break with silence, even as Cincinnatus was moved however reluctantly to break with the plow.

Sometime during 1968 we received at *National Review* the manuscript of an article, unsolicited and unheralded by the flacks of the literary world, from a young man, a graduate student at Berkeley, which took hold so firmly, and yet so unobtrusively, on what was going on at his university as to cause our small staff to marvel—gratefully—at the phenomenon. John Coyne simply related in that article, and in others that were to follow, what life was like at Berkeley, for himself and for others like him who found themselves unwillingly in the vortex of the unexamined surrealisms that have something to do with the revolutionary impatience that is gripping much of the student world in America.

John Coyne quickly attracted a considerable audience, distinguished (to judge from their letters) less by those who look merely for an additional reason to inveigh against the young revolutionists than by those who were truly grateful to someone who, by objective transcriptions of what was going on, gave us insight not only into the quite incredible lengths of what some of the students were doing, but into the far more unimaginable lengths to which so many members of a faculty formally committed to reason and meditation were disposed to go.

Upon reading this book, I am constrained to admit that the John Coyne of two years ago has changed. Here is the same sense of structure, the same remarkable powers of observation. But the detachment and distance of his earlier *National Review* writing have given way to involvement and perhaps even passion. Indignation has taken over, and, on the heels of indignation, alarm.

It is perhaps admirable to show sangfroid in every situation, and much great journalism is anchored on that principle. But Mr. Coyne's purpose here transcends the journalistic.

Since his first writings about Berkeley he has fathered two more children, and he obliges himself to consider the consequences for his family of six of a society that not only tolerates but seems to encourage the bestialities he was asked, at a university once considered among the finest in the world, to accept as a matter of course; asked by some to accept gladly, as the harbinger of a brave new world.

It is to put it lightly to say that his blood boils.

Maybe Lord Chesterfield could have managed to maintain his composure under the circumstances. Mr. Coyne chooses not to attempt to do so, and I think that he succeeds in making the point I have long wanted to see made: that there is a place for passion in public affairs—even from the right wing.

Here is a deeply felt denunciation not of the horrors of Stalin or Castro but of the quite inexplicable complicity of formally educated Americans with the travesties of the young brutalitarians whose passions, idealistic and neurotic, require, for their appeasement, the end of thought, the end of distinction, the end of such rational decencies as were taught us by Socrates, Aquinas, Burke, Mill, and Lord Russell the First.

Mr. Coyne implores us to look at what we have done to ourselves and our children and what our actions may mean to the future of our nation. I cannot believe that his *cri de coeur* will be ignored by readers who yearn for an intelligent and passionate guide to life in the revolutionary new societies that our universities have become. Or that the easy riders tagging along with the academic revolution who look into John Coyne's mirror will fail to discover how ugly they have permitted themselves to become.

The American riots of the 1960's baffled political historians for lack of a clearly defined purpose. More parochially, American political scientists and historians found difficulty in framing the perspectives of the new American forms of mass violence because of the set of American history. For generations, violence had threatened America most from the native American right—the menace always perceived on the lunatic fringe of reaction where Ku Klux Klan, American Nazis and Minutemen muttered, rumbled and mobilized as phantom marauders. But when the real marauders, in the 1960's, took to the streets, they came not from the "right" but from the "left" in the most liberal administration in history, while the thinkers looked the other way.

—Theodore White, *The Making of the President, 1968*

1

Add to Yale . . . the entire complex of the Western world's educational institutions, and you have in your grasp the nerve center of civilization.

—William F. Buckley, Jr., *God and Man at Yale*

This book is about Berkeley, where the New Left movement grew up in the last half of the sixties. Berkeley is the spiritual center of the movement, the Yenan in which it has slowly built its strength, refined its tactics, and made its plans for slouching in force to all parts of the country.

This is also a book about students, teachers, and universities in general. Few people, I think, yet realize just how central institutions of learning have become in American life. We know their influence and impact as research centers. Americans couldn't have walked on the moon without them. But the sociologic role of colleges and universities is still only vaguely comprehended. Theodore White pointed out in his last *Making of the President* that there are now nearly eight million American college students. And as they multiply, they are creating a whole new demography. Students have become the single biggest special interest group in the country.

The great chain of colleges and universities stretches across the countryside, each link a self-contained academic community, a self-governing city-state. As the demography of the country changes, the academic city-states become increasingly influential. Great gangs of

3

people have left the land to cram themselves into grubby cities, making them grubbier. And anyone who's ever climbed out of his cocoon and driven cross-country knows that as cities grow, smaller communities shrink. The New England woods, and whole great second-growth swatches of New York and New Jersey, for instance, cover numberless ruins of once thriving communities, settlements no one now remembers, nameless unpopulated places that archaeologists will one day puzzle over. Ladies in towns like Bellows Falls, Vermont, used to choose among dozens of daily trains to take them shopping in Boston. Now they either buy cars or stay home. Small towns across the Midwest slowly disappear as old grain elevators with their Copenhagen Snuff ads rust next to long-unused railroad sidings.

But as such towns and cities die, universities and their feudal towns flourish. In California, no sizable community lacks a campus, and each of these communities bases most of its economy and pattern of life on its college. Wisconsin, in addition to numerous private colleges, has at least a dozen state university campuses and rapidly is building more. Minnesota and Ohio and Pennsylvania add campuses just as rapidly. Even New York State, which usually lags behind the country in most things, has begun to catch on. This proliferation of colleges and universities creates new communities, revitalizes old ones. Iowa City, Iowa, for instance, once famous mainly for its mattress factory, is now the cultural center of the state. Philip Roth stopped by for a couple of years at the Writer's Workshop there. Touring dramatic groups, symphony orchestras, famous speakers come regularly, and everyone from the high school gym teacher to the owner of Osco's Drugstore knows at least as much about what's happening in the world today as, say, Clifton Daniel of the *New York Times.*

Universities have become our most important social institutions and, outside the narrow northeastern corridor, their satellite communities potentially our most important population centers. When these city-states, these nerve centers, become immobilized, a vital part of the nation is out of commission. When these city-states become radicalized, as has happened in Berkeley, revolutionaries find themselves in command of central training and staging areas that serve as jumping-off places for attacks on the rest of society.

Any high school graduate who can scrape through with a C is guaranteed college admission. The boys who a few years ago would have been driving tractors, pumping gas, selling ladies' underwear, are now stumbling along through Kafka and Shakespeare. And so they drudge on, the best of them, refugees from daddy's dry goods store in Crete, Nebraska, get their M.A.s and Ph.D.s, then move on to one of the new communities to spoon-feed another crop of students the same eclectic intellectual porridge that nourished them.

As the universities proliferate, they mass-produce at an alarming rate a whole new yet-to-be-classified class, and with it a whole new society, an educationist-technocrat complex, a loose confederation of city-states with centers in places like Normal, Illinois, Athens, Ohio, and Berkeley, California.

I spent a great deal of my life in these city-states, beginning in the early fifties, when, at sixteen, I entered Columbia University, having prepared myself for life in New York City by reading *The Great Gatsby* and *The Sun Also Rises.* A year later I enlisted in the Marine

5

Corps, did Korean occupation duty, worked construction for a while after discharge, then returned to Columbia. Had a few arguments with a couple of well-adjusted deans, developed a great distaste for much of the faculty, and finally quit. I transferred to the University of Alaska. And there, for the first time since the fourth grade, I began to learn something.

I had no politics, except for those reflex attitudes that I'd picked up at home. My father was a workingman who remembered what Roosevelt had done for him and invariably voted a straight Democrat ticket. I did likewise, of course, for the same reason that I still chew with my mouth closed. Like most of the students of the fifties, I tended to be apolitical, even, I suppose, "apathetic," as those college administrators who have since been chased out of their offices, had their wastebaskets defecated in, and died of heart attacks used to say about students. Apathy was a mortal sin to liberal educationists. They may have been right, of course. Perhaps what they called apathy was indeed a facet of devitalization. But it may also have reflected a form of relative stability. Who sneers anymore about those complacent Eisenhower years? Someday scholars may look back on the fifties as the last peaceful period in American history.

As I read and studied, I began to understand that every great writer, from Chaucer to Jane Austen up through Eliot, had one thing in common with the others. They all accepted as the standard for analyzing and judging character (and the analysis of character is what great literature is all about) a set of values that comprise the Judaic-Christian tradition and that glue Western society together. There have always been those who find meaning in the notion of continual flux and change. For them,

6

nothing is permanent, absolute values by definition cannot exist, since, in a universe in which things continually change, nothing can exist in one century in the same form in which it existed in the last. Yet literature disproves this, for Shakespeare's values are Jane Austen's. Just as they are ours.

There are values and standards of behavior that do not change, though we're often reluctant to accept their continuing viability. It's not really chic to do so. But we know that there is right and wrong, a correct and an incorrect way. All great literature, because it deals primarily with human behavior, must deal specifically with these standards of behavior, and all memorable characters in literature stand in some sort of definite relationship to them. They are universal values, values that can lift a literary work from the limitations of its own time in history and give it significance in all ages.

One can't explain the greatness of any art without granting the existence of absolute values. We admit their existence each time we read a book that is a hundred years old and thrill to what we experience in it. If we are impressed by Tom Jones, if we admire Jane Austen, if we are stirred by George Eliot, if we recognize in Dickens's characters people we have always known, what is it that we are responding to? If the relativists are correct, these works should merely leave us puzzled. Eighteenth- and nineteenth-century English spinsters and country squires, Shakespeare's kings and princes, certainly belonged to different tribes than we. Their mores are not ours, and what was expedient in life for them obviously is not expedient in life for us. Yet there is something we recognize and respond to—something that makes these works more lifelike and meaningful for us than most contemporary novels. We respond to a way of looking at things, a way of being and behaving in society. What is good for the character in the eighteenth-century English novel is remarkably like what is good for us today. His concepts of truth and justice are ours, and our standards of decency and morality are nearly interchangeable with his.

Through the study of literature I became a social and moral conservative. And inevitably, when it became necessary to think hard about politics, when at the end of the fifties the whole fabric of American society began to unravel, I discovered that I was also a political conservative. And this is not the most expedient thing to be in academe.

Academics are not quite like other people. They are extremely difficult to write about, for their manners and mores, if described faithfully, do not seem real. This is probably why most of the hundreds of novels written about universities seem so strained. The characters are often true to academic life, and for this very reason they look like caricatures living in small, highly mannered societies as orthodox and narrow-minded as old Salem. Such people, thinks the nonacademic reader, and such places just can't exist. But they do, and Cotton Mather would have made an excellent state university department head.

I thought about this the other day. I was sitting in my office at *National Review*, my feet up on the desk, drinking a can of Colt-45 Malt Liquor. And it occurred to me that it would have been absolutely impossible to put my feet up on a desk and drink that can of Colt-45 in any faculty office in any university in the country (except, perhaps, in the Ivy League—not malt liquor from a can, of course, but maybe a very small glass of dry sherry), even, say, at three in the afternoon, when many professors have long since finished with their daily hour or two of work and are either watching out the window for passing coeds or dozing over the latest little pleonastic piece cribbed from a couple of similar pieces and earmarked, eventually, for *Notes and Queries*. Even then, one couldn't open a can of Colt-45. It just isn't done. For those old reprobates, who between ogles delight in telling salacious stories to eighteen-year-old girl students, would as soon be caught taking a drink in their offices as they would in substituting a plug of Day's Work chewing tobacco for their pipes.

A farfetched example, but not unreasonable. And it tells, I think, a good deal about academics, the great majority of whom adhere just as rigidly to a fixed pattern of ideas as they do to customs of dress and deportment. Here are these classroom preachers of liberal orthodoxy, sneering for the edification of their students at evidence in any writer or thinker of what they like to call "middle-class morality," yet at the same time afraid to take a drink at their desks for the same reason that they don't pursue their classroom teaching to its logical conclusion and goose Mrs. Koslosky, the departmental secretary.

In academe there is generally one approved way of viewing everything: the codified liberal way. I remember once at the University of Denver listening to a couple of department heads discussing an applicant for a job. "Showed him the door before he sat down," chuckled one. "Can you believe it? He was wearing a *Goldwater* button." Gales of laughter, of course. Absolutely inconceivable that a well-qualified academic could support Goldwater. Must be a nut case.

And this is not unusual in the groves of academe.

Academic life is as carefully choreographed as Japanese No drama, each role requiring certain conventional responses, always automatic and on cue, with no room whatever for improvisation. This may explain the academic man's rather stupefying inability to make sense outside the academy (Arthur Schlesinger and Eric Goldman are two good examples). Nonacademics just don't know their parts. Before the first moon walk, for instance, I remember watching Marshall McLuhan on a network TV prelanding program, talking about space. Appearing with him was Bill Moyers, then publisher of *Newsday*. McLuhan clowned it up. The whole space program was rather silly, smirk-chuckle-chuckle, the term Sputnik was a *pun*, don't you see, smirk-chuckle-chuckle. And all the while he smiled that wry little smile, that ironical academic smirk that any student in the country would have recognized requires a good set of prolonged hee-haws, preferably in chorus. But there weren't any students around, and Moyers looked at him as if he were cracked. Which he may well be. Here was this archetypal academic, the quintessential contemporary professor, flawlessly performing the act that has made him the Captain Golly Gee-Whizbang of the academic world. But nobody got it.

And then, finally, he began to sense something was missing. Where were those appreciative titters, those knowing responsive nods of the head, those scribblings in the notebooks? No doubt he never quite worked it all out, but toward the end of the discussion, as he lapsed into complete gibberish, he'd begun to frown like old Welch in *Lucky Jim*. You could feel him itching to grab that red pen and give an F to Moyers, who failed to recognize the cues and persisted in talking sense.

I remember a professor at the University of Iowa who, like McLuhan, devoted himself to reducing the significant to trivia and elevating the inconsequential to universal significance. He was an old man, his face incongruously babyish under dirty white hair, his eyes blue and bright behind bifocals. I was still in love with the Victorians and the old man was reputed to be Iowa's best in that period, having at one time or another written a bunch of introductions to other people's essays that he then glued together into an anthology. (This is an important type of academic "research." One gets together a bunch of articles by others, writes a little introduction to each summarizing what the reader could just as easily summarize himself, and it is known henceforth as a "scholarly publication.")

The old man's seminar, open to graduates and advanced undergraduates, ostensibly was to be spent in profound discussion of Charles Dickens and Matthew Arnold. The real subject turned out to be his battle for the fluoridation of the water supply of Iowa City, a battle fought valiantly against "the forces of reaction," the "far right," epitomized for the old man by Goldwater supporters, of which I was one. (But "good old Coyne," they'd say, "he can't really *mean* it." If they think you're bright, you're simply not a conservative, no matter how often you insist you are.)

Now I *am* a conservative and I wouldn't even object to being called, in Whittaker Chambers's words, "a man of the right." But I really don't give a hoot in hell whether or not they fluoridate Iowa City's water. For all I care, they can fill the reservoir with bourbon and raspberry Kool-Aid. But I do object to having the whole ideological conflict reduced to terms such as these. And I strenuously object to the use of great literary works to support the small-minded partisan points scored by some little old professor in tennis shoes. And I object most of all to the academic comedy central to this sort of situation—all those bright kids, smirking and chuckling in appreciation of each simpleminded point, knowing that if they do not come in on cue those As or Bs will go aglimmering and those scholarships and fellowships will dry up.

And so this simpleminded old ideologue commanded a princely salary for spending a few hours a week reliving his battle for fluoridation. ("And how would Dickens feel about fluoridation?" he once asked.) Had there been a Students for a Democratic Society chapter at Iowa then, and had I not been a confirmed right-winger, I think I would easily have joined up and shoved a wastebasket over his head. (Last year, I learned from an Iowa sophomore honors student that he had found a new cause, something to do with liberalizing his church. He got kicked out of the parish, made *Time* magazine, and spent a year comparing himself to Martin Luther.)

Trivial, of course, silly, but perhaps it helps to explain why my heart went out a bit to George Wallace in '68 when he talked about "pointy-headed college professors." I was in Berkeley then, and the day after I first heard the phrase I watched a professor of history, his hair in his eyes and his face contorted with rage, trying to push into the Co-op Supermarket through the electrically controlled "out" door.

And it's not always that trivial. At times it's frighteningly profound, as one of these academic ideologues works diligently although not always consciously to break down the values students bring with them to the academy. The professor of a popular course at Berkeley in British literature was known to be a soft touch, meaning you could doze away the session, take no notes, write one of those subjective, top-of-the-head papers, scribble some sensitive little thoughts (preferably sexual ones) for the final exam, and get an easy B. An A came a bit harder, usually requiring the reading of a few introductions and the repetition on the final exam of some of the professor's choicer remarks.

He was fiftyish, short and plump, and he liked girls, pretty ones. They knew this, of course—the student grapevine is one of the world's finest intelligence systems—and they'd grab the seats down front in the auditorium where he lectured to a couple of hundred students, both graduate and undergrad. He'd lean over the lectern, gaze at the girls in short skirts, who'd stretch becomingly, and talk about "my wife's crumpled old body," which he'd compare with "your high breasts and firm thighs." Now, it's inevitable that the subject of sex will come up in any discussion of literature, but not necessarily in connection with every single work since the death of Victoria. One can perhaps forgive this professor his daily bout of rather mild self-titillation, but unfortunately it went a good deal deeper, debasing not only the poor goatish old professor but also the literature to which, presumably, he'd dedicated his life. By debasing the literature he debased the whole system of values that underlay the literature.

"Principles and values make us unhappy," he'd say, generalizing from the work under consideration. (It's an academic habit to use the occasion of analyzing the written word as an excuse to propound one's own eclectic view of the nature of man, the universe, and the local water supply.)

"Religion, nationalism make us unhappy," he tells

a bunch of kids, many of whom have recently left religious homes and are still, in their rather simpleminded ways, somewhat proud to be Americans. "Take care of matter and the spirit will take care of itself." But apparently it's no easy job to take care of matter, for the mood suddenly changes. "The only reality is the reality of loneliness," he says, staring at those thighs. "Man is trapped in a prison house of self and consciousness," living in "metaphysical isolation." Now he descends from the metaphysical. "Life is dirty and vulgar," he intones gloomily. Human existence is all "bestiality and cannibalism. . . . Remember that six million Jews died not long ago. Twenty-six million [sic] Ukrainians were slaughtered, and seven million [sic] citizens of Leningrad died of starvation. And here we sit listening to and giving a lecture on Virginia Woolf" (hardly, one wanted to interrupt).

"There is no authority in life or nature. Man is guilty of the general crime of being alive." (Guilty by what authority? one wanted to shout.) Man's duty is just "to drudge along." Why? Because "it's brave to live." Although, of course, in a world without authority and standards, bravery must carry the same moral weight as girl ogling, sodomy, or chicken plucking.

Thus it is in the "liberal" classroom at many universities today—the standard liberal-arts eclectic blend of liberal flummery, a half-cooked combination of the early-twentieth-century popularizations of Marx, Darwin, and Freud, stirred in with a healthy dose of the theory of relativity, imperfectly understood and dishonestly applied to human affairs. Add a pinch of existentialism, mix it all up, and watch the students get sick. How does one explain to these students that this posturing intellectual

14

pretender in jacket and tie lives the most orthodox of middle-class lives, the most nonconformist features of which are classroom ogling, brushing against coeds in hallways, and an occasional furtive trip to Whelan's Cigar Store to peek at the skin magazines while pretending to hunt for *The New Yorker?*

The brightest and the most cynical students know this, of course, and they play him accordingly. But do the more naïve know it's all just a game? What can there be to live for in a world of "bestiality and cannibalism," a world with no values and standards, a world in which the Sharon Tates are slaughtered as a matter of course? How about that confused girl from some hick town who loves her family and all they represent but comes to believe that their morality is artificial, their way of life hypocritical, their teachings baseless and corrupt? And how about that overly intense boy who gets the message loud and clear and follows it through to its logical conclusion by fire-bombing some campus building? I've seen it happen. Isn't his gesture essentially an admirable one, a gesture the professor, if he had any real convictions, would have to praise in the classroom, a blow for purity in a corrupt universe? Are teachers willing to accept responsibility for the rubble of these lives? Or will some professor shrug, as did Timothy Leary when one of his disciples, a teen-aged girl, drowned after an overdose of dope, and say, with Leary, why should I feel badly when so many people are dying in Vietnam?

What is this professor doing? For one thing, a conservative would reply, he's debasing the subject he's there to teach. Worse, of course, is that by using his subject to score political points he undermines the beliefs and traditions of many of his students. He is no Marxist, just

15

a typical liberal-leftist academic, and like most of his colleagues he probably has little idea of what he's done. And when those kids leave his classes, many of them with a whole belief system lying in rubble around their feet, they're prime material for conversion to a new system. And so, an endless crop of potential radicals for the special pleaders, the New Leftists. This is what William Buckley warned about in *God and Man at Yale.* And this is what drives conservatives from the academy. And the more we love the subject we want to be able to teach, the faster we go.

I discovered literature and conservatism at about the same time the country discovered John Kennedy, with his rhetoric of progress, movement, action for the sake of action. Many of us were agitated by this rhetoric, almost as if Kennedy were our generation's man on horseback. It was the time when the stability of the mid-fifties was giving way to a new instability. Something had begun to stir, something that made us vaguely uneasy, its shape not quite apprehensible. The beast was awakening.

On the campuses it was a period of transition. The last of the Korean veterans, who had changed the attitudes and set the life-styles for a couple of crops of students, were finishing up, to be replaced, in small trickles at first, by a new breed of very young and very intense activists. They came to free the Negro, to bring social justice to the world, and they took civil rights sabbaticals down south. Later they discovered the real abuses on the campuses and found that there was no need to travel all the way to Mississippi to right wrongs. The civil rights movement became the Free Speech Movement which became the Anti-War Movement which became the Anti-Everything-As-It-Exists Movement.

To us dinosaurs from the fifties, these were puzzling types, and we contented ourselves with drinking our beer and sneering at them. We didn't so much mind their intensity, for although the code of the fifties, like the code of all neoclassical periods, called for us to eschew enthusiasm, something way down inside us responded to it. But they were humorless, and we didn't like this at all. And they combined a great deal of worldly (although not necessarily experiential) innocence with a conviction that they had seen it all—which made us uneasy. They seemed uncomfortably like those true believers that Eric Hoffer had warned us about, touched, like all true believers, with a strong streak of uneducated fanaticism.

At the time, I no more recognized the potential shape of the rough beast that was then being born than did all those college presidents who welcomed them joyously, seeing in what they didn't understand an antidote to what they loved to call our apathy.

During the period that the beast had begun to move I applied to do graduate work at Berkeley, largely because I wanted to look at the New Left in its natural habitat. I was profoundly out of sympathy with much that I had seen in the academy, and I entertained a sneaking sympathy for the rebels, suspecting that their assault on the universities might well be justified.

This is always the danger, of course, when one gets things secondhand. I'd read diligently about the movement, but after a few months at Berkeley I realized that if you get your knowledge of the world from, say, essays printed in the *New York Review of Books*, you really

17

know only what is going on in the world of the *New York Review of Books*. The magazine essay has a well-established shape dictated by the formal requirements of written discourse. If you're going to write an article, you will need a beginning, middle, and end, with transitions and some sort of causal chain linking it all up. It must, in other words, hang together and make sense to the reader. Now, this is elementary, but it is also what makes essays misleading. For by imposing rhetorical order, which is, after all, an artificial order imposed from the outside, you make even the most formless and senseless subject coherent. All of which is a long way of saying, don't believe everything you read in periodicals. I'm afraid I tended to do so, and I thus arrived in Berkeley completely unprepared for the fractured, hysterical, mindless, and perhaps even evil nature of what I found when I got there.

I believed (and still do) that the university stood badly in need of reform. I didn't understand at the time, however, that the new revolutionaries had moved well beyond reformist ideas. Up to 1964, the movement had mobilized around such causes as amnesty for Caryl Chessman, the House Un-American Activities Committee hearings in San Francisco, the right of Malcolm X to speak on the campus, forcing the *Oakland Tribune* to modify its hiring practices, and so on. In those days CORE was still the center of radical activity. But then the Free Speech Movement erupted, and Mario Savio made his now famous statement of revolutionary principle. "There's a time," he said, "when the operation of the machine becomes so odious, makes you so sick at heart, that you can't take part, you can't even tacitly take part. And you've got to put your bodies on the gears and upon the wheels, upon the levers, upon all the apparatus, and you've got to make it stop. And you've got to indicate to the people who run it, to the people who own it, that unless you're free, the machine will be prevented from working at all." And so, the movement as it exists today. Its tactics have gone from protest to guerrilla warfare, its aims from reform to destruction of the whole machine.

Things were temporarily in disarray when I landed at Berkeley. Mario Savio was in jail, Bettina Aptheker was pregnant, and the various radical groups—the SDS, the Young Socialist Alliance, the Progressive Labor party, the Independent Socialist League—were thrashing around desperately for stirring causes and coherent issues. I watched them stage confrontation after confrontation, gradually picking up sympathizers despite dozens of clownish failures, the various groups growing more unified until they congealed into what we now call the New Left. And as I watched it grow the alarm bells began to ring. This was something unique in the American experience, going much beyond legitimate student protest. It was an attack on the basic framework of American society. The Berkeley New Leftists were (and are) attempting to destroy the university, and the university has become, I believe, for better or worse, the central social institution of contemporary American society. If the university falls, as it presently gives indication of doing, other less stable institutions will follow quickly.

I hold no brief for the present corrupt condition of the American university. But the way to reform a corrupt institution is not to blow it to oblivion, which is what the New Left set out to do, often with the tacit consent of teachers and administrators.

There has not been since 1860 a time of such na-

19

tional danger and tension. The excesses on the campus are spreading slowly but steadily into society at large, and at the same time a very real wave of very hard reaction has begun to gather momentum. Not a bad historical analogy in more ways than one is Weimar, Germany, just before Hitler took over.

If we are to halt the present process of disintegration, those of us still capable of enough concern to try to salvage America must do our best to understand what's happening and why. The place to start is the university campus, and there's no better campus for openers than Berkeley.

2

As a citizen, the professor's freedom is limited in the same way as . . . other citizens—it does not embrace . . . inciting riot or any exemption from the laws. It also carries with it certain limits set by professional honesty and decorum.

—Richard Hofstadter

My feelings about Berkeley, California, have always been ambivalent. It's a lovely place, one of the loveliest in North America, a place, one writer recently pointed out, you get addicted to. It's also an unusual place, unlike anything in the American experience. A whole new society has grown there with a unique set of manners and morals and a new sensibility.

Recently, on a gray, airless, muggy, grimy, sooty, jostling, snarling typical Manhattan afternoon, as I waited on a Fifth Avenue street corner for a green light, over the cacophony of horns and New York-cockney cabbie screams I heard tambourines. Hopping and whirling down Fifth Avenue came some members of the Hare Krishna cult, chanting their pidgin Buddhist chants, mostly young Caucasians with shaved heads and saffron robes.

I'd seen them often in Berkeley, where they, like so many similar groups, had originated. I hadn't liked them at all, for there seems something peculiarly sick about middle-class American kids who freak out on the mindless passivity of Oriental pseudomysticism. But on that afternoon, as I watched them come down Fifth, with all of Manhattan gawking, I heard some over-thirty meathead observe profoundly, "Christ, look at them silly bastards."

I wanted very much to punch him. As a conservative I should of course agree that these were indeed weirdos; but as a Californian I very much resented an eastern provincial boor sneering at what passes for near-normal on the West Coast. Cults are part of the California way of life. What has become commonplace in Berkeley is still only beginning to stir around in the rest of the nation. New York has its East Village, to be sure, and the clothes and the manners and the politics are patterned on Berkeley. But it's still not quite natural back here, and when you wander through the East Village you feel they're just acting. "Hey, man, look at us," they seem to be saying. "Aren't we *different*." In the East they still are—perhaps explaining the inability of easterners to make sense of California.

Periodically, a writer will be sent out to the West Coast by an eastern magazine to write it up. He jets to San Francisco or Los Angeles, grabs a cab to a hotel, soaks up a few days' worth of booze, then jets back east to explain California to the rest of us. And we get the same old string of clichés that everyone has used since Nathanael West. But the clichés are completely misleading, for the writer inevitably treats what he sees as an aberration, while, given the California context, it's all perfectly natural. What seems aberrant to the easterner —the Hare Krishna cult, for instance—is simply an integral part of the society, a new and radically different society that has grown up almost imperceptibly inside the older, more traditional one and has just about taken over. There's an old cliché that California is five years ahead of the rest of the nation; travelers from the past to the future seldom can make sense out of what they see.

I feel no great love for the new culture (except, of course, when New Yorkers sneer at it). And many of the things associated with it, I believe, have made possible the growth of such groups as the SDS. But Berkeley is the seat of the new culture, and I do love Berkeley.

Take the weather, almost impossible to describe to a New Yorker or a Chicagoan or a Pittsburgher. The sun is different, even in winter, large and warm, almost a tropical warmth, but the heat is always cut by a steady Pacific breeze blowing through the Golden Gate and across the bay to Berkeley. The air is delicious, tangy, and when you return after a stint in a place like New York you can eat it. And the sky on the western rim is bigger and much, much bluer, sharp blue. The days usually are extremely bright, colors always primary, never eastern pastel. Long days, and there's no twilight; up to the moment that the sun drops abruptly into the Pacific it's nearly as bright as noon. Foliage is multicolored and exotic, especially on the university campus, easily one of the most beautiful in the world. Hundreds of varieties of flowers, blooming year-round. Tulip trees, rose trees, purple trees with purple leaves, palm trees, giant eucalyptus trees with peeling buckskin bark giving off their oriental oily smell.

And there are the kumquat trees, among the branches of which street people and hippies often take their breakfasts.

Life is easy in Berkeley, and people live outdoors, which is partly why the campus is usually so crowded. Thousands of people—students, faculty, nonstudents, New Leftists, street people, tourists—daily pass through Sproul Plaza, an area about the size of a football field, bounded on the west by the Student Union Building and cafeterias, on the south by Telegraph Avenue and Bancroft Way, on the east by Sproul Hall, the administration building, and on the north by Sather Gate and the Kumquat Grove.

The plaza is the center of things, and on any given day its western edge is lined with folding tables behind which advocates of causes ranging from the recall of Governor Reagan to the abolition of leash laws shout out their arguments at passersby. Noontime is show time. At twelve the bell ringer begins a midday concert from the top of the campanile (I always expected a hunchback to come swinging from the bell tower and carry off a coed in a peasant blouse). The campanile is centrally located, about a hundred yards east of the kumquat trees, just back of the main library and most of the office buildings. The terrific din effectively empties most of the buildings; the inhabitants usually wander over to the plaza to catch the show.

The plaza belongs to the radicals at noon. The administration, a few years ago powerful enough to prevent Adlai Stevenson from speaking on campus, by 1966 had become so tangled in its own intricate diplomatic concessions that it found itself providing the New Leftists with not only a stage (the steps of the administration building) but also a high-powered public-address system, complete with a battery of microphones, dutifully set up each day by university maintenance men. All is the exclusive property of the New Left. I once saw a small group of conservatives try to hold a noon rally on the steps. As they moved toward the microphones, a group of Negro thugs, street people, and SDSers blocked their way, threatened them with violence, and shoved them down the stairs. There were about six conservatives (a phenomenal number for Berkeley, nevertheless) and about fifty of the others. The conservatives were all students who had reserved the microphones well in advance through the dean's office. Perhaps ten of the people who chased them off were students, the other forty Telegraph Avenue-West Oakland types. The conservatives complained, but of course the administration did nothing. This is the last time I can remember in nearly two years that conservatives attempted to exercise free speech. Free speech at Berkeley means freedom for New Leftists and their sympathizers *only*.

It was on the plaza that I had my first good chance to watch the New Left in action. One day in October, 1967, when I was still gulping the place in and nothing seemed too serious, a battalion of New Leftists marched up Telegraph and onto the plaza.

The bell concert had just begun. On the lower plaza a rock band blasted away at a bunch of Berkeley high schoolers. Evangelists screamed. Jug bands tooted. The Hare Krishnas chanted and twirled beneath a huge picture of their leader, out of whose nostrils grew long spiky black hairs. A couple of Black Panthers scowled and strutted around near the microphones while their women shrieked.

The New Leftists tramped toward the Kumquat Grove, several hundred of them, chanting, "Hell, no, we won't go." And as if to prove it, they wheeled around just short of the kumquats and marched back. Out in front strode a girl in Levi's, a tight sweater, and no bra. As she walked she bounced, much to the delight of a small pack of black militants close on her heels. Behind the braless girl and her admirers tramped the New Leftists, most of them in denim jackets and dungarees, flashing the peace sign. They wore wild frizzy hairdos and bushy beards, and as they marched they grinned happily. A few fraternity types, trapped between the campus coffee shop and Larry Blake's Telegraph Avenue beer parlor, stood and gawped. Dogs danced and snarled among the bare feet. Tweedy professors nodded paternally and chuckled at no one in particular. Evangelists screamed louder, the bands blared, the bells began "Standing Somewhere in the Shadows You'll Find Jesus" (or something), and a few hippies woke up. The New Leftists occupied the Sproul steps and began to outline to the crowd their plans for closing down the Oakland Induction Center. And I loved it.

I'd just escaped from the Midwest. My perception of what was going on was almost entirely superficial, and this silly-looking New Left army seemed no more menacing than the Three Stooges. But a few weeks later I realized that the New Left had decided to move off campus in force, to go to war in earnest with American society.

It had been building.

An organization called Stop the Draft Week had gradually grown from the Anti-Draft Union, controlled by the SDS, to something called the Resistance, broad enough to encompass all the leftist groups at Berkeley. (As of this writing it's the New Mobe.) And by early autumn they believed themselves finally strong enough to move out in force.

Things had been kicked off by the professors. Various published statements in support of draft evaders had been drawn up at Princeton, Harvard, the University of Wisconsin, and Stanford that spring, and in May two hundred Berkeley professors, along with faculty from other California campuses, had issued the following declaration: "We believe our war in Vietnam is immoral, unjust, unconscionable. . . . We believe that every young man has the obligation to choose for himself whether he will train to kill and perhaps be killed in this war. The decision of conscience cannot be made for him by any external authority, including the American government. We therefore urge young men to consider whether they are willing to be executioners and victims."

Now, I don't know how you feel about Vietnam. But I do know that there are many honest people with honest doubts about this war, just as there are many honest people who honestly believe we cannot in good conscience simply walk away from it. But there is no room for this latter view in the faculty statement, which makes it clear that the opinions of those people who believe our pursuit of the war an honorable one are "immoral" and "unconscionable."

This single-sighted arrogance, this inability to see another point of view, more than anything else makes the conservative fear the academic leftist-liberal. What do the professors here say to students they presume to guide and counsel? The student has a free choice: he can either agree that the war is immoral or he can join the "executioners." He can, in short, fight on the side of the angels or the side of the demons. There is not the slightest hint that it is possible to support the war effort without being bloody minded.

Consider what is urged. A moral decision about the war is made. Having handed down this decision, the teacher now exhorts the student to make a "decision of conscience," to defy the "external authority" of the "American government." The student is urged, in other words, to break the selective service laws. Now, while the present selective service system is a defective patchwork, sometimes blatantly unjust (until recently, for instance, there were deferments for students and none for union apprentices) and often zany, it is nevertheless a system based on law, and when you violate this system you break the law.

Nothing more insidious has developed in the academy in this decade than the almost total acceptance among liberals of the notion of "selective" lawbreaking. Such good men as Martin Luther King did, to be sure, select certain bad laws to break. And there are bad laws. But there are also bad men like Lee Harvey Oswald and Sirhan Sirhan who also selected laws to break that no doubt they believed to be bad. In the end it boils down to a choice of which laws to break and who should break them. If northern professors advocate breaking selective service laws because they find them immoral, why shouldn't southern politicians advocate breaking civil rights laws, which they just as sincerely believe to be immoral? And why not murder any man you find to your moral satisfaction to be evil? Isn't, in his case, the law against murder an immoral one?

It is this absolute faith in his own rectitude, this willingness to set up as arbiter of absolute morality, this dogmatic belief that only his view is just, that today's conservative finds most frightening in today's liberal.

Some of the faculty signers of the antidraft statement were old standbys—Professor Richard Lichtman, for instance, and New Left counselor John B. Neilands, professor of biochemistry, who took time off from his university duties to act as a member of the team investigating war crimes committed by the United States for the International War Crimes Tribunal run by Ralph Schoenman, Bertrand Russell's protégé (Schoenman was later denounced as a charlatan by Russell and now, presumably, has to earn his living). Others, who realized as the year dragged on that the government was expressing an

increasing interest in prosecuting those who actively
encouraged draft resistance, quickly stopped signing petitions. While there is an odd inability among liberals
to see the eventual broad consequences of their
actions, they do have a good sense of their own
best interests. But by the time they disengaged themselves, the damage had already been done. Planning
for a massive disruption to shut down the Oakland Induction Center began soon after the faculty had issued
its statement. The target date was October 16 to 21, and
the leftists had been traveling the country, coordinating
plans for universities elsewhere to hold supporting demonstrations on those days. (One mystery yet to be solved
is where the New Leftists get their funds to travel ex-
tensively from campus to campus and city to city. They
number among the steadiest customers of United States
airline companies. And this in addition to the massive
amounts of money they constantly put up for bail and
legal defense.) The aim of Stop the Draft Week, according to Michael Lerner, Lichtman's protégé, was to mo-
bilize "massive civil disobedience" by rioting in such
cities as Oakland.

On October 11, five days before the sit-ins were to
begin, the university, at the behest of the faculty and the
SDS, named Stop the Draft Week a legitimate university-
recognized organization, just like the yearbook and the
Inter-Fraternity Council. (It takes months to get a conservative organization recognized at Berkeley.) SDS then
applied for use of the Student Union for "an anti-draft organization center." The Student Union would, according
to the student newspaper, be used "as an embarka-
tion point for proposed anti-draft activities at the Oakland Induction Center." As an afterthought, the professors tacked onto the SDS request the statement that

31

there would also be "an all-night teach-in." (Which there wasn't, unless you consider that calls to riot are teaching.) "The teach-in idea," said the student paper, which supported the mobilization, "was conceived to allay the administration's fears that the meeting would have no educational purpose."

In the meantime, the Alameda County Board of Supervisors, unwilling to see Oakland turned into a battleground by invading students and nonstudents who were not only non-Oaklanders but in many cases non-Californians, demanded that the university administrators prohibit the use of campus buildings as staging areas for the disruptions. The Stop the Draft Week organization, said the supervisors, "is a registered university organization and is using and proposes to use University facilities in furtherance of its illegal activities." Dean of Students Arleigh Williams scolded the supervisors: "Students have the right of advocacy just as you and I have the right of advocacy." (Notice this strange inability of the academic mind to distinguish between lawbreaking and advocacy, the same inability that doesn't allow it to distinguish 'between indoctrination and disinterested teaching. One of the crucial reasons, perhaps, why the whole notion of academic freedom has become so bizarre.) "The administration can't, doesn't want to, and ought not to control the content of what people say," announced Professor Robert H. Cole of the Berkeley Law School in 1967. Take note of "say," and then catch "therefore": "Therefore, it has never been a policy that people cannot organize on campus for illegal off-campus activities." Which gives the Mafia, apparently, the right to use the Student Union to organize its white-slavery rackets.

Chancellor Roger Heyns tried similarly to soothe

the supervisors. "As for the avowed intention [to rip Oakland up] of the group to which you refer, recent history here and elsewhere [??] shows that there is likely to be a vast difference between announcements and action." What recent history? Where? When? What other announcements? Actions? Heyns sails along majestically: "It is a common technique to announce outrageous or illegal acts." Common? Among whom? And where? "These may not occur due to careful educational work on the part of more experienced and thoughtful people."

And how were these "more experienced and thoughtful people" (the faculty, in other words) carrying on their "careful educational work"? Well, Professor Richard E. Willis of the History Department told students that "if the law is seen as embodied evil, it becomes necessary to break it . . . demonstrators who advocate defensive violence are . . . justified" (this, of course, is precisely what Sirhan thought). On jump-off day, Professors Lichtman and Neilands stood before five thousand cheering students and read a telegram that began: "War greetings to progressive Americans." It came from Hanoi. And others of the "more experienced and thoughtful people," members of the Academic Freedom Committee, issued an official faculty resolution that went in part: staging sessions on campus are "fully consistent with University and campus rules governing University facilities, the U.S. Constitution, and with the basic doctrines of academic freedom adopted by our faculty." Thus, a whole new pack of definitions of academic freedom. For Heyns and Dean Williams, the freedom not to perceive what's going on. For liberal professors, the freedom to be impulsively irresponsible. For the Academic Freedom Committee the freedom to use the campus as a base for attacking neighboring communities. For Professor Willis, the right to play vigilante. For Professor Cole, the freedom to use the campus as a staging area for illegal activities. And for Professors Lichtman and Neilands, apparently, the freedom to use the campus as a base from which to fight for Hanoi.

Not too surprisingly, then, the Alameda County supervisors were a little less than reassured, and on October 16 they had an injunction issued that forbade "the use of University grounds, facilities, or buildings at any time by groups or organizations . . . for purposes of on-campus violations of the Universal Military Training and Service Act and on-campus advocacy of off-campus violations of said act."

This cut no ice with the New Left, however, or, for that matter, with most of the campus inhabitants. A typical response, printed as an editorial in the student paper, reads: "We must say 'no' to the Alameda County Board of Supervisors who would prohibit our teach-in program." The same paper, a day or two before, had admitted that the whole teach-in notion was just a sham to keep the administrators happy. "We support the program and urge that everyone who cares about academic freedom and the future of this university attend. . . . The people of California have already made a mistake in trying to dominate the university with their own views."

This typical view goes a long way toward explaining why Californians so distrust the university. Oakland is just another city with little real connection with Berkeley. But there's an induction center in its downtown section, and for this sin thousands of radical university types and their allies proposed to rip the city up. The people who live there didn't want it to happen, naturally, and they found it particularly upsetting that the University of California, an institution that could not operate without

34

their tax money, tacitly and often actively encouraged this disruption. Galling for taxpayers to discover that their tax money pays for attacks against their community. Galling that few of the attackers themselves pay taxes, and galling to be told that the attacked have no right whatsoever to protest. No academic freedom for the people who pay for the academy.

And so, on Wednesday, October 17, five thousand New Leftists, old leftists, students, nonstudents, street people, and dogs marched into downtown Oakland. They burned, smashed, and managed, as Mario Savio had advised, to stop the machinery. True, they were effective for just a few hours. But during those few hours they were very effective indeed, and the New Leftists enjoyed the first real taste of their potential power. They also managed to find a new enemy, the Oakland Police Department, an enemy that was to figure heavily in later confrontations. The police, naturally enough, had attempted to contain the demonstration, and in so doing had been forced to use their clubs. (Not really, after all, anything more than an application of Professor Willis's concept of "defensive violence." The police were, after all, the attacked, the defenders. But police are not allowed "defensive violence." They're not covered by academic freedom.)

There were 317 arrests, and after the violence the university administration tried to wriggle out of any responsibility. Chancellor Heyns, properly aghast at what those "more experienced and thoughtful people" had wrought, attempted to prove that the university had had little to do with it all, since only a few of those arrested were registered students. Apparently forgotten by Heyns was the "teach-in," the active faculty encouragement, and the use of the campus as a base for the invasion, a use,

35

once the precedent had been set, to which the Berkeley campus would increasingly be put. And of those arrested, Heyns neglected to mention that many were former students or nonstudents active in New Left movements who used the campus as their headquarters and hotel.

Stop the Draft Week was a literal failure, since the draft was not stopped. But it was a great success in the long view. The university had provided the New Left with a secure base, and once such a concession had been made the administration was to find it impossible ever again to control the campus. The radicals had mobilized a broader support than they had enjoyed since the Mario Savio days, and although this support tended to drop off following each new battle, they knew that it would appear again once they'd found a broad enough issue. And they had found one fine subissue, always effective, in the action of the Oakland police. Much of the rest of the academic year was taken up with rallies deploring police brutality. And they'd discovered that they could effectively terrorize communities larger than university campus communities, a lesson they put to good use in Chicago the following summer. The invasion of Oakland was, in many ways, a rehearsal for the invasion of Chicago. The New Left had managed to switch the tactics completely from protest to confrontation, and the country would never be quite the same again.

And so, in 1967, the University of California at Berkeley declared war on American society, and other members of the university network stretching across the country were soon to join up. They went to war under the banner of the Vietcong, the legitimacy of their cause primarily supported by the concept of academic freedom. And pity the professors who started it all. The revolutionaries grow younger each year, and the poor professors find themselves increasingly on the other side of the generation gap.

For my part, as 1967 ended I was still feeling my way around, still in the first stage of that developing love-hate relationship with Berkeley that will probably last for as long as I do. The Oakland invasion didn't touch me the same way later battles were to. It wasn't until 1968 that I became personally involved.

3

Anyone who hates children and dogs can't be all bad.

—W. C. Fields

The excesses of Stop the Draft Week dampened the enthusiasm for disruption among many students, and the winter and spring quarters passed fitfully. There were rallies, plans for raising defense funds for the students arrested in Oakland, and occasional scuffles. But for the time being the heart had gone out of the movement, and radicals seemed to be talking only to themselves. The New Leftists grew increasingly edgy, until finally, in early July, a series of spontaneous street riots erupted. These were important to the New Leftists, as it later turned out, for they resulted for the first time in an alliance with the street people, the several thousand neo-hippie drifters who have taken over southeastern Berkeley.

A jumble of impressions. I remember walking along Telegraph Avenue in the summer of '68, toward the Hofbrau, the finest place in Berkeley to sit and drink Carlsberg and look out at the Telegraph street scene through the large windows that front the avenue. As I walked I breathed in great gulps of the tear gas that still hung in the air and the tears ran down my face.

I remember too that summer an outfit called the Women's League for International Peace and Freedom, which held a "violence workshop" on campus shortly

41

after the riots had ended. Mrs. Elsie Boulding, a sociology teacher at the University of Colorado, pointed out that members "of the white middle class have been conditioned into believing that if we all get together and talk about it, a solution will be found. It isn't true." The middle-class academics, who were sitting around talking, chuckled. "We must surrender being totally realistic," chimed in Berkeley political science professor Sheldon Wolin, New Left apologist who declares that violence isn't really violence at all (except when committed by right-wingers). "The events of the last few decades have shown us that realism has had its day and has brought us close to the edge of disaster." And then the panelists sat down to a good middle-class box lunch. With soft drinks.

It was also during the summer of '68 that I first began to notice the dogs. Across Sproul Plaza and through the cafeterias and classrooms roams one of the largest stray dog populations in the world, snarling, defecating, fornicating, and cadging meals from outdoor lunchers. This population has grown in much the same way as the street people-New Left population, and the campus and the surrounding community have reacted to them similarly. That summer the New Leftists had for a brief period effectively closed the campus and the administration had confessed it was unable to curb them; Larry Schmelzer, head of something called, in typical university fashion, the Environmental Health and Safety Department, had at the same time admitted to a similar inability to control the dogs. Schmelzer claimed that the stray dog situation was so bad it would take a full-time crew three months "to reduce the unlicensed dog population to reasonable levels."

The city of Berkeley also suffered. In early July the

New Leftists successfully linked up with the swarming street-people, Telegraph-Avenue culture, and together they had terrorized the city for several days, breaking windows, burning, and smashing, until the City Council had to declare a state of emergency. Citizens were irate, knowing that after a raid the marauders could retreat to the sanctuary of the campus, where they'd regroup and hold mass meetings to plan the next raid.

The dogs did likewise. Daily they'd roam off the campus, pad through food stores and restaurants grabbing snacks from counters and plates, defecate and urinate on the carpets in the Bank of America, bite shoppers, and then retreat to the campus when the dogcatchers appeared. The City Council, unable to get the New Leftists locked up, took on the dogs by introducing a proposal for a stringent leash law. The reaction was predictable.

"If you love dogs or believe in freedom, speak against the leash law," urged the student paper, which later ran a picture of an adorable fuzzy little puppy reported to have been exterminated by the humane society, along with a piece about the assistant director of the society calculated to make him sound like Heinrich Himmler. "If I cannot afford property," stated another student, "I cannot have a dog," thus linking stray dogs to class warfare. "Dogs have long been a part of this campus," wrote a typical academic, "exemplifying a spirit of freedom."

There were the reactionaries, of course, among them an official of the Student Health Services who recognized the striking similarities in the life-styles of street people and dogs: "It may seem amusing to watch the dogs steal lunches from unwary students but it is pitiable when you realize that this is the only way these dogs stay alive—

by the lunches they steal, the garbage cans they raid, or the handouts they can mooch by begging or scare tactics."

A professor of zoology, in a letter to the student newspaper, complained that dogs regularly attended his classes and that recently two of them had proceeded to mate as he lectured. And I remember a class I was attending in which the professor had just launched into a dramatic discussion of the Leda-and-the-swan myth. He flapped his arms in the air, swanlike, and shouted, "Here came this great beast!" And a yelping setterlike bitch came running through the door pursued by an amorous shepherd. They raced up one aisle, down another, and behind the lectern. The professor scooted around the table, waving an eraser, shouting things like "heel." The shepherd took a nip at him, missed, then followed the setter outside. Later in the year the same class was disrupted by student activists who forced the professor to cancel his lecture.

Striking similarities, in several ways. Back in 1965, for instance, when the student movement was still essentially reformist, a graduate student named Donald Halock was eating his lunch at the outside cafeteria on the plaza. Each time he forked in a mouthful, a pack of stray dogs around his table snarled and yelped and lunged. Finally one of them jumped onto the table and sank his muzzle in Halock's food. Halock grabbed the dog by the scruff of the neck and dropped him over the railing ten feet to the grass below. This prompted the following letter to the *Daily Californian* from an onlooker: "The puppie's [sic] screams and cries did nothing to arouse further interest in the student [Halock] but did draw interest from witnesses to the atrocity. The student refused to accompany the animal to the hospital, stating, 'I must finish my lunch.' Your act, Donald Halock, was despicable and unfathomable [Halock claims he tried for five minutes to chase the dogs away]. The fact that you are a graduate student perhaps lends more shame to your crime. Your utter lack of interest in the pain you caused an innocent animal to suffer indicates inhumanity and an incapacity to love." The next day a veterinarian reported that the dog had received no injuries.

The letter writer's reaction is essentially the same reaction, prompted by an undiscriminating and hyper-emotional sensibility, as that of the now-defunct civil rights movement, that do-gooder mode of feeling that every northern college girl took with her when she traveled down into Mississippi to liberate all those nice Negroes.

The strain of sensibility has been passed down to the new revolutionaries, and their revolt is less rational than emotional. But it's sappy-nice no longer. I remember a chilling moment in early 1969, just before massive police squads hit the campus for the first time. The New Leftists had turned tough and mean, the tactics now paramilitary. It was a cold gray evening and I was hurrying toward Doe Library, having just watched a band of New Leftists punch and kick a skinny boy who had tried to raise some dissenting points at one of their meetings. I felt sick. Suddenly, over near the Kumquat Grove, a dog began to keen in a hysterical, high-pitched way. A mangy shepherd had a student backed up against a tree and was ripping at his legs. A large group of people stood around, unmoving, until finally a girl somehow managed to pull the dog away. "You gotta stand still," said one onlooker. "Probably kicked him," said another. "Poor dog," added a third.

Odd. For it seemed to me that just at the time the

radicals became vicious, the dogs tasted human flesh. And discovered yet another delightful aspect of their freedom on campus.

Freedom for dogs? Exaggerated, but symbolic. For it is the set of mind, the tendency to react in predictable fashions, the often ludicrous inability to make meaningful and sensible distinctions, that has made the university so vulnerable to the attacks of the new anarchists. This fuzzy inability to distinguish the significant from the absurd, in fact, might serve as a workable negative definition of the whole notion of academic freedom, a notion capable of infinite expansion under which the most aberrant ideas and actions can be nurtured.

The summer of '68 was the summer of the dog. It was also the summer of the beast.

The Drama Department decided to produce Jakov Lind's play, *Ergo*. Lind, an expatriate Austrian who describes himself as "sharp, anti-right-wing Barry Goldwater," sees capitalism as the source of all evil. To dramatize this, he makes his play a study in sexual deviation. The villain is a "capitalist pig" and, of course, a kinky pervert. The hero is a socialist. The action of the play consists of a series of sex acts, ending in an oral-genital orgy. The performers were students and faculty.

Such a play would usually cause little comment at Berkeley, or for that matter on most liberal campuses. But there was a foul-up. Professor Hardin Jones, a medical physicist and one of the very few faculty conservatives to survive at Berkeley, went to see *Ergo*. "I have never known of any performance, on or off a university campus, of such morally destructive and depraved character," wrote Professor Jones to the *Berkeley Daily Gazette*. "Sex actions occurred throughout the play . . .

these acts were pornographic, brutal, sadistic, inhuman, and insane." He pointed out that the performance was paid for by taxpayers and organized by a teaching division, and asked: "What responsibility does the university have for the fact that students acted out these depravities, indecencies, sacrileges?"

The academics were flabbergasted that one of their own would be vulgar enough to mention values, morality, and faculty responsibility. But the Board of Regents rather liked his point, and in one of its resolutions expressed "deep concern over the lack of propriety of recent dramatic presentations and productions on university campuses, and particularly on the Berkeley campus" and instructed "the president and the chancellors to take whatever steps may be necessary to assure that future campus productions conform to accepted standards of good taste and do not portray lewd, indecent, or obscene conduct."

Now, most people outside the academy—lovers of New York theater and skin movies excepted—probably wouldn't find this resolution too oppressive. All the regents were asking was that the Drama Department not insist its students fornicate or perform perverse sex acts on stage for university credit. But this, of course, is a commonsensical view, and common sense is not prized in the academy. The reaction was predictable. Henry May, head of the Drama Department, labeled the resolution a "violation of academic freedom."

And then the attack on Professor Jones began. Professor May stood before the Academic Freedom Committee to defend the play and to slander Professor Jones, who asked to appear before the committee but was not invited to do so. Academic freedom protects New Leftists, Black Panthers, deviates, Communists, and dogs.

But it does not extend to conservatives, Professor Jones. Jones even supported Max Rafferty, California's controversial Superintendent of Public Instruction, for the U.S. Senate. Openly. So Professor May and the Academic Freedom Committee decided not to give him a hearing.

Professor Jones was used to this sort of treatment, however, and he decided to go ahead and try to make sense out of it all. "The point at issue," he said soon after the blast from May, "is whether academic freedom gives license to the faculty to direct students in the performance of acts of indecencies." He pointed out that "acts of simulated sexual intercourse were portrayed by students under faculty direction. Presumably there were also tryouts for these parts. One wonders here just what qualities the faculty looked for in the young female drama students. One also wonders what sort of a grade a girl would get who refused to subject herself to these indignities. And according to Professor May's own statement, the students performed for credit and were graded."

And then Professor Jones revealed that "in one simulated but realistic sexual act, in the beast position, the male role was played by a member of the faculty."

One can only hope that the girl at least got an A.

The concept of academic freedom covers a multitude of sins. But perhaps nonacademics will agree that the line really should be drawn somewhere. Surely it's just a bit thick to insist that academic freedom means the freedom of faculty members to act out their goatish fantasies with the active assistance of students. But then, academic freedom is a complex concept. Especially so, now that it covers the beast position.

The summer of '68 also saw poor Professor Lichtman scrape bottom. He was consistently, as I have mentioned, a most eloquent New Left supporter. He is a widely respected teacher, his course in Marxism being one of the most comprehensive and best taught at Berkeley, and in 1968 he was voted "Teacher of the Year." It's tempting for a conservative to try to assert that, given his biases, Lichtman couldn't help but brainwash the students who took his course. But I have no evidence that this is true. I do know that his course seems most popular among the already converted. I also know that the course is brilliantly constructed and extremely well taught.

But in the early seventies, perhaps classroom indoctrination means much less than it used to, for politicized professors such as Lichtman no longer confine themselves to the classroom. The campus at large has become the classroom, and professors label their giant rallies "teach-ins" and claim that their speeches serve an "educational function." Thus the academics now expect the cloak of academic freedom to cover their extraclassroom activities. And thus they can be charged with indoctrination as well on the Sproul steps as in any classroom. And there is no better mass indoctrinator than Lichtman.

He is eloquent. "There is something basically corrupt with the American power structure," he said on one occasion to a large campus audience. "Our imperialism in Vietnam is not incidental. The system is basically evil . . . the Vietnam war happens to be the current vehicle of that system." It's not the war that's bad, as the sincere critics contend, it's the whole system that's rotten. The war is just a symptom of the larger sickness.

At the same meeting Lichtman urged students to disrupt a scheduled CIA recruiting visit. "The CIA coming is not a matter of free speech [this in response to the notion that even representatives of government agencies should be covered by the First Amendment] but recruitment: an abominable system of recruitment to murder." The temperate, dispassionate rhetoric of the academic, uttered under the cloak of security provided by the concept of academic freedom. And the students disrupted, of course. Prominent among the disrupters were students from Lichtman's Philosophy Department. One of them, Miss Wren Leach, a senior philosophy major, won some instant fame by lying on the ground in front of campus police and screaming, "Don't touch me, don't touch me." They didn't, but her performance was effective enough to allow the SDSers to shriek about Gestapo tactics and storm the building in which the interviews were being held.

Another occasion: an on-campus "teach-in," at which a SNCC representative explains that there's no difference between Wallace, Johnson, Reagan, and Bobby Kennedy. Pigs. "You got to get yourself some guns," Black Panther Emory Douglas tells students. John Seeley from the Center for the Study of Democratic Institutions, where they've apparently decided we could do without such institutions, points out that *all* administrations are corrupt and that "we can't allow this [the system] to go on." Robert Scheer, formerly of *Ramparts,* sums up much of what is going on by saying that "to be reasonable is to be irresponsible." Ralph Schoenman shouts, "The system is a global system. Without victory over it there is no survival." And finally there is Professor Lichtman, calling upon students to "bring down the university" so that the system of which it is a microcosm can also be brought down.

At another rally Lichtman says the American system is "a system we have to bring down." And, lest there be any doubt, "This isn't a game." At yet another gathering, this time an on-campus debate between Lichtman and students for Kennedy and McCarthy (Kennedy and McCarthy were considered conservatives at Berkeley), both candidates are "bankrupt and morally corrupt," announced Lichtman, who supported the Peace and Freedom candidate, convicted rapist Eldridge Cleaver. American domestic policy he described as "murder by starvation." Then, directly to those impressionable students who hang on his every word, "You don't change the structure of American society through the university, the party structure, or the rules as they come down to us. You have to work outside the rules. I think students have recognized the necessity for this." Indeed they have. Every time a building blows up, every time students riot under the Vietcong flag, they prove their lessons have sunk in.

But in the summer of '68, Lichtman was gloomy. The wide-scale destruction over nothing in particular during the Telegraph riots of early July had deeply angered nonacademic Berkeleyites and those students who were not yet politicized. The radicals argued and quibbled, and it seemed for a brief while as if their nonideological support, always necessary for staging successful confrontations, had vanished for good. It was against this background that Lichtman and his fellow speakers attempted to raise spirits by speaking at the July 16 Solidarity with Cuba rally.

Each speaker did his best. The first to mount the Sproul steps, a graduate student, explained how the United States had "exported Jim Crow to Cuba." Fidel had solved the problem, however, by leading "an integrated movement." If we integrated, he concluded, we could cure racism in the same way Fidel had. Black and white together, we could overthrow the government. This brought a lot of applause.

The second speaker, who seemed to have spent much of his life roaming from campus to campus to stir things up, was more fiery. He urged the Berkeley students to get the hell off the campus and start tearing everything down. Berkeley, he shouted, reminded him of pre-Fidel Cuba. "The Cuban stoo-dents talked a lot but then went off and did their own thing, like being doctors, undertakers, and what have you," he declaimed with a sweeping gesture. General applause, but less enthusiastic when he ended by telling how Fidel put the poets and homosexuals to work in the cane fields.

And then came Lichtman, who had just arrived from Cuba. He had been struck, on his return, by the American air of "self-indulgence." (As he said this he patted his developing paunch, no doubt unconsciously.) But it was "joyless" self-indulgence. A major difference, in fact, between Americans and Cubans was this quality of "joyousness." Cubans are joyous, he explained solemnly, even when queuing up in their long ration lines after a hard day of cane chopping. (He admitted that he hadn't talked to those people in the queues. But he's a philosopher, and therefore no doubt able to sense joyousness wherever it exists.)

The listeners seemed a bit less than joyous, but Lichtman plowed ahead. He began to explain how Cubans get into the Communist party. They're admitted, he said, only if their entire lives show "deep seriousness" and "earnestness." The image of joyous Cubans being joyously serious and earnestly joyous troubled me, since I'm a nonphilosopher, but then Lichtman cleared it all up by pointing out that Fidel had created a new man, a man who couldn't be analyzed according to any standard concepts.

Lichtman next described the characteristics of this new man. He differs from us in all ways, perhaps the most important being his sense of time. In the United States everyone lives in the present. (Except for us simplistic right-wingers, of course, who live in the past.) But in Cuba everyone lives in the future. For the future, Lichtman lucidly pointed out, is right now in Cuba.

Professor Lichtman concluded by celebrating the joy of honest toil, much to the delight of half a dozen construction workers who were sitting on the Student Union steps, eating their sandwiches, and watching the coeds. Americans, he said, just don't understand the value of hard work. (This was especially stirring, coming as it did from a teacher of philosophy. One antisocial type in the crowd, who in the interest of free speech was quickly shouted down, said something about there being no calluses on Lichtman's small pink hands.)

Lichtman concluded by urging us all to get out into those cane fields.

4

White liberals, in their hunger for humiliation, will take as revealed truth anything an angry black man says.

—S. I. Hayakawa

The Vietnam war had proved an excellent issue, but after the '68 riots it temporarily lost its appeal for many of the Berkeleyites. The radicals, if they were to be effective in future confrontations, had a problem, part of which was the need to encourage students to accept at least some of the wider view—that the Vietnam war itself was just a symptom of the rottenness of society— of such academics as Richard Lichtman. This view is probably accepted now by a good number of students. But a couple of years ago, despite intensive indoctrination, it still seemed extreme to many. The war was, after all, relatively remote, being fought for the most part by noncollege types without deferments in a distant land. It was still probably more of a faculty cause than a student one. (Not until 1969, actually, did the New Left finally succeed in developing a broadly based coalition of antiwar supporters.) And then there was the whole political situation: the candidates of both major parties were obviously going to try to change our war policy.

But perhaps the biggest damper of all had been the assassination of Robert Kennedy. Those students not yet ideologized, the most honest among them, realized a very basic fact: their disruptions, the violence the New Left had unleashed, had created an atmosphere in the United States that made such acts possible. Speakers on campus had long defended violence, and the call to get guns and use them had become common. Let no one forget that after Kennedy was murdered the New Left pictured him in one of its publications as a dead pig.

There was, in other words, that climate of hate and fear that the liberals are forever accusing the right of creating. (I remember the first TV newscast I watched after John Kennedy's death. The commentator announced that he'd been shot by a "right-wing extremist." Later, when the broadcasters found out who and what Lee Harvey Oswald was, they minimized his leftist connections and blamed the whole thing on the climate of hate and fear produced in Dallas by rightists.)

Extremism in any form was temporarily out of favor at Berkeley, and so the New Leftists had to scratch around for a more direct and appealing issue, one that would bring kids and the professors back into the fold. And they found it, finally, an old issue really, hanging around from the civil-rights-protest-do-gooder period. The issue was racism. It was an issue that was to crystallize around Eldridge Cleaver and eventually tear up the campus and reduce Berkeley, which in 1966 had been named by the American Council on Education the "best balanced distinguished university in the country," to what may well be permanent second-rate status. And, perhaps most important of all, it was an issue that was to lead to a powerful alliance between New Leftists and black militants. The new alliance, a combination of New Leftists, ideological professors, street people, and black militants, was to give the disrupters the troops they needed to fight the big battles.

Black activists had long been wary of New Leftists.

During the Ronald Reagan-Edmund G. Brown guberna- torial campaign, for instance, when the SDSers had tried to get Negro support for their anti-Reagan drive, the head of the Afro-American Student Union had said at a Sproul rally, "The SDS people will just shave and go back to New York if their strategy backfires." But at the same time the new mood was growing, perhaps best summed up in a *Negro Digest* article by J. Hermann Blake, a Negro writer. "I remember sitting before a TV set last year and cheering each time a building in Watts erupted into flames. . . . Perhaps the brothers in all the ghettos will one day realize that we should not just have cheered Watts, we should have joined them at the same time in our own cities."

And on the campuses they were on the move. At San Francisco State, fifteen Negroes stormed the office of *The Gater*, the student paper, and beat the editor and his staff. They destroyed typewriters, overturned desks, scattered files. The editor, Jim Vaszko, was taken to a hospital. A professor visiting the office was also beaten. The Negroes were not punished (punishment is a sim- plistic right-wing notion). At about the same time a group of blacks, most of them nonstudents, physically prevented a small group of conservative students from holding a scheduled rally. One of the Negro students involved, Jim Nabors, explained, "I've been denied so long that anything I take is right." The academics agreed. None of the blacks were punished for blatantly violating university rules. And an anonymous Black Panther put it this way to Berkeleyites: "There will be no more rocks and bottles. Now it's hand grenades, dynamite, and ma- chine guns" (and not long afterward it was revealed that Negro militants at San Francisco State were using funds collected from student fees to buy automatic weapons).

"It's going to be a blood bath," he continued. And listen carefully, do-gooders: Social work, community projects are "too little, too late. We're not interested in patchwork—we're interested in revolution."

Symbolic language, the liberals tell us. They just *talk* this way in the ghettos. They don't really *mean* it. But the violence had begun. At Merritt College, six members of the student government resigned because of assassination threats made by militants with the encouragement of a faculty member. And on a bright December day they hit the campus of the College of San Mateo in a chilling action that was for some reason scarcely mentioned in the national press. One hundred and fifty Negroes had held a noon-hour rally at San Mateo. The speeches were impassioned, and the crowd chanted and screamed and danced, working itself up to a savage pitch. Non-Negro onlookers grew increasingly uneasy and began to drift away. Suddenly, with incoherent screams of rage, the Negroes began to race across the campus. They pulled metal water pipes from the ground and used them to smash windows and to beat horror-stricken students and faculty. One boy, his head cracked open by a pipe, was carried off to a hospital in critical condition. A girl was thrown down a flight of stairs and her face ground into broken glass.

"I don't know whether they wanted to kill or destroy," said the badly shaken president, Robert Ewigleben, who had been punched in the nose. "But the last thing they wanted today," he continued, putting it as only an academic could, "was to open up communications."

The terror unleashed at the College of San Mateo set the tone for demonstrations across California. Sit-ins developed into demonstrations which developed into riots which developed into guerrilla warfare. At San

Francisco State, administrators and many faculty members became accustomed to threats on their lives, and on at least three occasions their homes were fire-bombed and shot up with semiautomatic weapons. Places such as San Fernando Valley State College, the College of Vallejo, prestigious institutions such as Stanford, all came to accept life under almost daily siege. At San Jose State, blacks ran through buildings, breaking up classes, beating students and professors. At Berkeley a white athlete walked out of a campus building and was shot by two blacks. And down at UCLA, deep in the heart of Reagan country, traditionally the quietest of the state campuses, what everyone was dreading finally happened. Two black students were murdered on campus.

Against this background, Eldridge Cleaver decided to move his headquarters from Oakland to the Berkeley campus. And he was invited to do so by the university.

The summer of '68 had finally ended. Rioters had burned down a house on Telegraph Avenue, smashed most of the glass in the community, both on and off campus, blown off part of a building, and shot a policeman. The Berkeley city manager declared the whole of Berkeley a disaster area.

Nevertheless, the administrators, apparently mistaking a temporary cease-fire for a truce, overcame their combat fatigue in early September and again began to speak with that odd unfounded optimism so peculiar to educationists. On Friday the thirteenth of September, Chancellor Heyns was addressing a group of VIPs gathered in Harmon Gymnasium to eat supper and listen to speeches celebrating the university's centennial year. And as the chancellor got to the part about how the activists had finally quieted down, and how the campus was in for a tranquil year, the gymnasium was rocked by

61

an explosion strong enough to break the crockery. Someone had just blasted the nearby Naval ROTC offices with a homemade bomb.

A timely explosion, symbolic of things to come. Just a couple of days before, the university had set off a bomb of its own, when a rather fuzzy-headed public relations man had announced that Eldridge Cleaver, at the time minister of information for the Black Panther party and candidate for President of the United States on the strangely named Peace and Freedom party's ticket, would teach a course for credit on campus. The course would explore, said the announcement, "the dehumanization and regeneration of the American social order." The subject matter was vaguely described as "racism."

The shock waves rolled quickly through the state. Governor Reagan, who doesn't enjoy diplomatic recognition at Berkeley but does represent a majority of California voters (honest, he really does), predictably voiced the majority opinion: "Perhaps on the heels of a campus Vietcong rally, the Vietnam commencement [a masquerade party, held in June, at which faculty handed out make-believe diplomas to New Left draft dodgers], and other recent performances . . . I should not have been surprised. But I am." And even liberal Jesse Unruh, Reagan's archenemy, was shocked. The university, said Unruh, seemed to be expressing a "death wish."

The furor really shouldn't be too hard for nonacademics unfamiliar with the notion of academic freedom to understand. First, on the most basic level, there was the matter of Cleaver's criminal record, a record to which he continues to add. At the time of the announcement of his appointment, he'd already done time twice, once on a narcotics conviction and once for rape, assault to commit murder, and assault with a deadly weapon. And in September of '68 he was awaiting trial on another charge of assault with intent to kill (this was the charge that eventually caused his exile). Such a record, especially when its owner shows not the slightest desire to reform, isn't usually the kind that gets you hired for a teaching job, as Regent John Cannaday attempted to point out when quizzing one of the professors responsible for setting up Cleaver's course. "In any of your other courses," he asked, "have you brought in outside lecturers who are rapists and felons?"

And then there was his position in the Black Panthers. In '68 they still seemed, to many people, no more dangerous than a Sons of Italy drum and bugle corps. A restaurateur used to greet Cleaver and cronies at the door of his establishment with "You be good little Panthers now." They seemed to do a great deal of posturing and strutting about, they dressed up in striking costumes, but all they really accomplished was to pick up white college girls, get their pictures in national publications, and shoot themselves with their own weapons. Others, mainly at that time law enforcement people, viewed them differently. The Panthers were arming, they told scoffing liberals, they'd already been involved in several shoot-outs, and they'd murdered an Oakland policeman. And when they learned to handle those weapons they were collecting, the police believed, they intended to start armed uprisings in the cities. The Panthers didn't deny this. Their official newspaper proclaimed it to the world. But of course the liberal academics simply didn't believe them.

Cleaver himself was one of the foremost advocates of violence. In a talk to a group of San Francisco lawyers, for instance, a typical talk of the sort he gave almost daily around the Bay Area, he spelled out the Panthers' aims: "If we can't have it, nobody's gonna have it. We'd rather provoke a situation . . . that will disrupt cities and the economy so that the enemies of America could come in and pick the teeth of these Babylonian pigs." During the question-and-answer period he was asked what others could do to help. "Kill some white people," he replied. And he meant it. Less regeneration than dehumanization here. Straight from the Panther's mouth. I doubt that any parent—left or right—would be eager to deliver his children up to such a "teacher."

His appointment must seem incredible to those outside academe, the most charitable view being that academics simply don't understand what's going on in the world around them. They preach social involvement, of course. But they live comfortably isolated in handsome homes hung up in the Berkeley hills, where Negroes cannot afford to live. And so their social interests are anachronistic. For liberal academics it's still 1938 and Franklin Roosevelt is still in office. They've lost touch, and since an Eldridge Cleaver doesn't fit into their picture of things, they just create an Eldridge Cleaver of their own.

Finally, and belatedly, the academics tried to justify themselves. Cleaver, they claimed, would not be paid with university money after all. His salary would come from some rather mysterious "outside sources." Reagan wasn't appeased. "I don't really care whether they're printing the money to pay Cleaver in the basement over there," he said. "It is on the university campus. It is a course for which five units of credit will be given. As far as I'm concerned, it is a university program."

The university then tried arguing that Cleaver was uniquely qualified to teach a course in which the subject of racism would be central. This brought another Reagan snort. "I don't know why they never asked the head of the American Nazi party to conduct a course on racism," he said. "It would be a very interesting course. It could even get into the area of science—how to build an oven, how high a fence around a concentration camp."

Unable to make any sense, the academics decided to try nonsense. The faculty was stirred out of its summer doze, the specter of the other Senator McCarthy, the one from Wisconsin, was called up, and the old battle cry of academic freedom rang out again. Academic freedom was being violated, they shouted. Whose? Well, they hadn't quite worked that out yet, and they never really did, but specifics were unimportant. What was important was that the university had finally thought up a way to let itself off the hook, much like a girl caught in a lie will begin to cry, and suddenly you're the one in the wrong. And so, faced with this flood of tears, the Board of Regents overrode Reagan and narrowly voted not to demand that the university rescind the Cleaver appointment, not wanting to face a pack of academics all worked up over the issue of academic freedom. No man, after all, relishes the prospect of dealing with a weeping woman. But the regents did vote to allow Cleaver one and only one classroom appearance. No great hardship for those students dying to hear him, for he made his home on Sproul Plaza and could be heard there shouting about shooting fascist pigs almost any day of the week.

The regents' compromise ended by pleasing no one at Berkeley. Cleaver and his followers took it as part of the plot by the pigs to sell them back to the plantation owners, and the university became as much their enemy as the Oakland police force was. The faculty was all whipped up, and academic emotions aroused over academic freedom do not subside easily. And the people of California, the taxpayers, were outraged. About the only happy ones were the New Leftists, who, after spending the previous few months scratching around for an issue, had one served up to them on a platter by the university.

And so, as the explosion that kicked off the centennial celebration presaged, it turned out to be a great year at Berkeley. The only people who suffered were the taxpayers and the students. But that didn't break any academic hearts. What was important, after all, was the academic freedom of the black racist and campus Panther, Eldridge Cleaver.

The course itself never got off the ground. The regents' September 20 resolution, limiting Cleaver to one lecture and denying university credit for the course, pretty effectively killed it. But only as a course, and not as an issue. The New Left beat the drums, and there were daily rallies at which such professors as Lichtman pointed out that the regents' action proved the university and therefore the country at large were not only fascist but also racist. Fires raged around the campus and through Berkeley; bricks sailed through library windows (try to read your Jane Austen with bricks sailing by your ears).

Many of the faculty at first seemed not too unhappy with the regents' decision. They get nervous, after all, when an outsider who wears no tie, no tweed jacket, no pipe, no degrees, is admitted into their fraternity. Had the intruder been someone like Max Rafferty, say, they would have sided completely with the regents. But this was a Negro, and liberal faculty love Negroes, who remind them of Sidney Poitier movies. And besides, academic freedom was the issue, wasn't it? And so, in the faculty club, at departmental meetings, they played on one another's nerves and grew increasingly edgy.

The first responses seemed, nevertheless, slightly tentative, cautious, and the odds were about even that they'd do nothing rash. "If you're going to have a Dreyfus case," said one professor, "you'd better be damned sure your Dreyfus is innocent." But as September moved along, good sense increasingly gave way to near hysteria. The New Leftists further clouded the already murky issue by building it into a Ronald-Reagan-versus-free-speech battle, and the faculty, many of whom had used their classrooms as a forum for attacking Reagan during the '66 gubernatorial campaign, grew steadily more willing to do battle. And so, finally, the professors decided to do something. They called a meeting of the university Academic Senate for October 3, a meeting in which they ended by deciding to oppose the Board of Regents.

The faculty came up with a resolution urging those who were putting together Cleaver's course to go ahead with it as planned. But they also adopted an amendment that directed the faculty to "consult with the Chancellor, the President, and the Regents, for the purpose of re-scinding the Regents' rulings." Now, there was as much chance of getting the regents to rescind their ruling as of converting Max Rafferty to Buddhism. But it's a comment on the faculty view of the world that they believed it possible. And the reaction of the militants was predictable. They were enraged that the faculty would consider negotiating with the regents and they were bitter that the Academic Senate hadn't insisted on a specific room assignment for the course. The faculty had compromised, and after October 3 they never again exercised any real power at Berkeley.

The faculty compromise meeting took place late in the day on October 3, a strange day even for Berkeley. It began with a series of false fire alarms set off by SDSers. Fire trucks rolled across campus, blocking off pedestrian walks, and militants spread the rumor that it was all part of a plan to suppress the noon rally, at which Cleaver was to be the chief speaker. Many classes didn't meet, and those that did were sparsely attended, mostly by people who insisted that the professors talk about racism (today, especially in the liberal arts departments, most classroom lectures at Berkeley center around this sort of thing). By the time the bells in the campanile began to smash and clang their noon concert, the campus was unusually jumpy. Students, ex-students, nonstudents, dogs, New Leftists, hippies, street people, bums, Berkeley high schoolers, perverts, pickpockets, TV cameramen, lunatics, tourists, professors—the typical campus crowd —several thousand of them, filling Sproul Plaza from Bancroft Way to the Kumquat Grove, milled around waiting for Cleaver.

Cleaver is an impressive man, especially when he has a five thousand-plus audience, all sympathetic. He always comes late, part of the act. On October 3 he was about half an hour late, and the crowd had worked itself up to an explosive pitch. You could feel him coming. A strange low moan ran through the crowd and then people began to applaud. A corridor opened and Cleaver came into sight, sauntering along, unsmiling, surrounded by a half-dozen Panther bodyguards in black leather jackets and black berets, casing the crowd and talking into walkie-talkies. Cleaver walked slowly to the mikes, gave the clenched-fist salute, then led the crowd in three choruses of "Power to the People," followed by three

"Fuck Ronnie Reagans," each chorus louder than the preceding one, delivered in unison, much like those chilling *Sieg Heil*'s they used to shout at the great Nuremberg rallies.

I was standing very close to Cleaver as he gave his brief, obscene talk, and his face fascinated me. It's a Mongolian face, one that could have belonged to a member of the hordes that rode out of the eastern deserts to pillage and torture the effete Europeans. His eyes are slanted, narrow and slitted, hard eyes, dead and cold, the eyes of a killer, and as he talked about killing Reagan (you could feel what pleasure it would give him to do so—perhaps the only thing left in the world that could give him any real pleasure) those eyes flickered back and forth over the crowd. And they were contemptuous, deeply so as the crowd responded in a definitely sensual way, girls flushed and squirming and shrieking and boys mindlessly screaming approval as Cleaver coldly talked about killing whites. This mindlessness is frightening, the sexuality sickening. Cleaver played on the sick sexuality and found those people who responded to it contemptible. An evil man, a rapist and a killer, whose warped mind has managed to project its sickness into society at large and give shape to a revolutionary movement. But a man.

Cleaver played on the crowd, working it up, but stopping just short of orgasm. And when he finished and left abruptly, the crowd, five thousand strong, seeking relief, marched toward Wheeler Hall, the building in which the Berkeley faculty was due soon to assemble. They jammed around the building, shouting and chanting obscenities, and the first of the professors who had begun to trickle toward Wheeler stopped in their tracks, quite

69

obviously frightened, perhaps believing that the revolution they'd been calling up for so long had finally broken out.

Some of them turned back, but then a strange thing happened. The crowd wasn't throwing things. It was actually applauding them. The teachers didn't believe it at first, of course, and they looked wildly about them, wondering who in the world was causing the applause. Then it began to sink in. The mob opened aisles for them through which they had to pass to get inside Wheeler, much like captives running Indian gantlets. The first of them were scared as they hesitantly followed their pipes down the aisles. But each in turn was given a rousing ovation, and they began to relax, some of them even flashing the New Left victory sign. (There's an awful lot of ham in most professors.)

It had been a long time since Berkeley professors had been offered affection by students and, coming as it did, it had the same effect as a shot of bourbon on a reformed drunk. The pipes puffed more fiercely, the tweedy shoulders squared, the faces flushed with pleasure, and the sidelong glances they threw at the crowd grew increasingly paternal. These were their students, by God, their *children*, and they were daddies off to even accounts with that big bully, Ronald Reagan, who'd been picking on them. Nearly every professor at Berkeley walked that emotional gantlet on October 3, and by the time half of them had passed through, the whole business had become so blurred that they'd forgotten all about the real Eldridge Cleaver. It was all fathers and sons now, academic freedom having become the right of daddy to protect his kids. (The president and the chancellor, incidentally, entered Wheeler through the back door.)

As the meeting began, the professors obviously were emotionally sky-high. Someone, perhaps that same bubble-headed public relations man who'd handled the initial announcement of the Cleaver course, had decided that the mob should know what the faculty was doing in there and the faculty should know how the mob felt about it. So two-way sound equipment was set up. The crowd could hear every word uttered in the auditorium, and the professors could hear the reactions of the crowd outside, This blunder, an innocuous action in itself, was perhaps more than anything responsible for the Berkeley professors' losing the last of their waning influence.

It began like any other faculty meeting. But not for long. For whenever some professor fumbled around with *Robert's Rules of Order*, the roar of outrage from outside caused audible nervous grumbling inside. And whenever someone like Professor Kenneth Stampp, one of our most famous and respected American historians, tried to inject some reason into the debate, tried, in fact, to find out just what was being discussed, the mob simply hooted him down. ("Who the hell's this Stampp?" grumbled one student.) Another professor tried to argue that Cleaver would be a bad influence on students already badly ideologized. A refugee from Nazi persecution, he was jeered because he spoke with a German accent.

Others, however, such student favorites as Richard Lichtman, were cheered lustily. Lichtman delivered a fiery speech exhorting the professors to lay it on the line and vote for direct confrontation with the regents. Lichtman was riding high, and his colleagues were very careful to hear him out, although they quickly cut off doubters like Stampp. (And as soon as Lichtman finished, disciples such as Michael Lerner circulated through the crowd, selling pamphlets written by the professor for 50 cents apiece.)

The discussion inside never really got off the ground. There was no real debate, for the mob didn't allow it. One professor tried to appease everyone by trying to explain just how the regents' resolution violated academic freedom but ended by getting all balled up in the Bill of Rights and the French Revolution. Another pointed out that the faculty had no legal basis for defying the regents (which they didn't). He was ruled out of order. And several professors tried to question the academic validity of the Cleaver course. They too were hooted down.

And so, without understanding what they were doing or why they were doing it, the professors decided to vote on a motion to defy the Board of Regents. The haste was, of course, caused by the amplified noise of the mob. It was also precipitated in a rather comic (or, depending on your point of view, tragic) way by a sudden announcement from the chair that the auditorium had to be cleared so that the janitors could put it in shape for "another university function." The janitors may be the second most influential group at Berkeley, a little less powerful than the New Leftists but a good deal more powerful than the faculty. And so the faculty decided to hurry the vote, despite the pleas of Chancellor Heyns, who begged them to wait a day or two until emotions subsided. To his credit, Heyns was one of the very few academics who saw the day for what it was.

They voted hastily, adopting a resolution that was a direct attack on the regents in that it demanded the course be given just as originally planned. But it failed to appease the radicals because it did not insist that a room be assigned immediately for Cleaver to lecture in. And so, when the professors filed out, proud of having done their duty by the children, they were stunned to find the children jeering them.

"Shame," came the shout. "You fucking cowards," they screamed. And the professors looked as if they wanted to cry. The pipes went out, the shoulders slumped again, and they scuttled off for home, perhaps to think for the first time about what they had done. For in the heat of emotion they had opened the door for the regents to crack down. And they had handed the New Leftists an excuse to arrange bigger and better demonstrations.

President Charles Hitch, making an unusual appearance before the Academic Senate earlier in the day, had delivered a telling argument for restraint. "With few exceptions," he pointed out, "our moderate support throughout the state has disappeared. . . . There is a widespread feeling that the university is somehow bent on its own destruction. I used to think that statements like this were fatuous, but I find now that over one course, or, more accurately, over one man, there has arisen an issue which really could destroy the university as we have known it."

President Hitch's remarks proved prophetic. On October 3, the professors had demonstrated that they were incapable of running their university. The "academic freedom" of the campus Panther was insured, but Berkeley would never recover. The regents in the following months steadily took back those privileges they'd previously granted to the faculty, and the daily business of the university increasingly was conducted in Sacramento.

And on campus, the New Left took over the reins from the academics. After October 3, the New Leftists inherited the University of California at Berkeley. Their new issue, combined with the Vietnam war, was racism in the person of Eldridge Cleaver, whose Peace and Freedom party had built itself on both issues. The university itself was racist as well as imperialist, Professor Lichtman now pointed out, just like the whole rotten society, and from October 3 on every new confrontation was billed as "antiracist."

There is very definitely racial discrimination at Berkeley; examples are legion. At the beginning of the fall quarter of 1968, for instance, militant members of the Afro-American Student Union decided they needed some office space. So they marched to the fifth floor of Eshleman Hall and took over rooms occupied by five student organizations, among them the health services. They emptied desks, broke open filing cabinets, and threw documents out into the hall. Those responsible for room assignments simply shrugged it all off, and the deans suggested that the ousted organizations go elsewhere. Normally, such an incident would have administrators climbing the walls, expelling students left and right. Not in this case.

Such incidents are routine. One day I was prowling around campus. (At this point, a word in my defense. It may seem as if I spent all my time sneaking about the campus, Pepys-like, with my little notebook. Perhaps I did. But there wasn't much else to do. Classes either didn't meet or met only to be disrupted or met to allow professors to give their views on whatever happened to be going on on the campus at that particular moment.) And as I was prowling around the Sproul Plaza card tables, I was handed a mysterious document. Put out by the campus unions that comprise junior faculty members, graduate students, clerical workers, librarians, it was a thickish document entitled *The Union White Paper on*

74

Racial Discrimination in Employment at the University of California, Berkeley. It could just as well have been called "The Final Solution to the Caucasian Problem."

It was a racist paper, racist in tone and diction as well as intent. When it spoke of Caucasian administrators, for instance, it called them "lily-white." (People aren't "midnight black," "chocolate brown," or "rose red." Only "lily-white.")

The proposed solution, like all great plans, was simple and direct. "There should be," the unions said, "about 8,000 more black-brown-red [sic] faces on the Berkeley campus—2,500 more employees, 6,300 more students." To bring these multicolored faces (along with their bodies, one hopes—Berkeley is already bizarre enough), the unions demanded "that only black-brown-red [sic again] persons be hired." The university was urged, in other words, to violate the Civil Rights Act by hiring people of certain races. And no Caucasians need apply. Not even those California Caucasians with sunbaked brown faces.

One could argue that there just weren't that many people around with black, brown, and red faces who also had the training necessary to step into administrative and teaching jobs. The plan spoke to this objection, however. "The University of California," it commanded, "shall establish free on-the-job training programs aimed at upgrading minority-group employees." If qualified people with black, brown, or red faces couldn't be rounded up, then forget the qualifications and take the faces and let the university teach the faces to do whatever they're supposed to do. Should the university suddenly find it needed someone to teach a Shakespeare seminar, for instance, it should not hire a Caucasian replacement.

What it must do was go get a red, brown, or black drop-out and teach him all about things like the procrastination controversy in *Hamlet*.

Some of the stodgier academics, mainly a few conservative professors, tried to raise the question of standards. But this was just a Caucasian dodge. Academic "standards of expertise . . . function as the legitimate rationale for illegitimate racism." Clear? The typical composition course was a case in point. "Language standards taught in composition courses reflected a white middle-class cultural standard and usually generate penalization on minority cultural patterns in language."

It's easy to satirize the New Left, partly because of their unbelievably dogmatic humorless arrogance (and it tells you a lot about the militants that they think Jerry Rubin is funny), partly because of their mindlessness. Their whole notion about racism is almost completely ludicrous. Almost. But not quite. For, fools like Rubin and madmen like Cleaver to the side, they've almost got hold of something. There is indeed something cockeyed about the way the universities are treating Negroes.

The real villains are the professors. They stand solidly behind integration immediate and total for society at large. But at Berkeley they suggest autonomous black studies departments, staffed by and run for Negroes and Negroes only. Just keep them out of our departments, the professors say.

Up to a point one can understand the reluctance of professors in many subject fields to accept large groups of Negro students, most of whom come to universities such as Berkeley from urban slums, in the schools of which they often never quite learned to read. What they stand in need of is not courses in physics or Continental literature but basic remedial reading and writing and talking courses. The solution certainly isn't to stick these students in classes that would inevitably have to be watered down to accommodate them. And it certainly isn't to institutionalize their flawed education by setting them apart in schools of black studies.

Remedial education, intense remedial training, is the most direct need. In addition, there is plenty of room for Negroes at places like Berkeley in technical programs that demand much less than the straight academic ones. Almost all black activists claim they're seeking an education that would be relevant to Negro needs, an education that would equip them to return to the slums to help the people there to better themselves. But every proposal for a black studies school that I've seen seems to focus on courses such as Negro history and Negro literature. What possible use would a black literary critic be in the slums of Harlem or West Oakland or Watts?

On the other hand, a black librarian would be beneficial indeed. Consider, for instance, the Library Science School at Berkeley. Its curriculum is very straightforward, the courses no more difficult than the professors try to make them.

Now, to get a good job in a library, you must be a "professional" librarian. In other words, you have to get a credential from one of those schools, such as the one at Berkeley, that are accredited by the American Library Association. And where are librarians needed desperately right now? Right down there in the slums, where those Caucasian ladies who push the Bobbsey twins are not loved at all. But they're still mainly the people who get the credentials.

And why aren't there black librarians helping their

kids to learn to read and write and think? No credentials. Why? They're not getting into the library schools. Why? The professors don't want them there.

And so there's Berkeley, bordering the Oakland Negro slums, boasting the only accredited library school in the immediate area. It's a big school, several hundred students. And at this writing only *one* Negro student, who's dutifully trotted out and displayed by the dean whenever he's asked what his school is doing for civil rights.

Racism is rapidly becoming the central issue in society at large as well as on the campus. I've spoken about what seems to me a deadly sort of reverse racism practiced by black militants, championed by the New Left, and cheered on by the professors. This new reverse racism, this attempt to set up a neosegregated society that operates on a set of double standards, is insidious. Like nothing else before, it threatens to tear up society—and undo completely a couple of decades of improving racial relationships.

I think of the way things were in other parts of Berkeley. There were places like the Berkeley Square Tavern, for instance—handsome, with deep padded leather chairs, carpet, padded bar stools, fireplace— where they pour good big drinks at about a third of the cost of similar drinks in New York. The Berkeley Square is on University Avenue, just west of the railroad tracks, almost exactly at that point where the white community runs west into the black. There's a mixed clientele—old-time university people, Berkeley merchants and their wives, barbers and tailors, workingmen who in the East would seem out of place in such a bar. And a few years ago, Negroes from much the same classes.

Black neighborhoods have expanded rapidly in West Berkeley, and some of the slums are almost as bad as eastern slums. But between Sacramento Avenue and the Berkeley Square, running north to Albany, the adjoining community, there's a great residential stretch of middle-income housing, which was once solidly white but is now about evenly integrated. The houses along this stretch are mostly small, neat Spanish stucco houses (the dominance of Spanish architecture in northern California always surprises outsiders), which seem always freshly painted, the sharp green lawns looking as if they'd been trimmed with barber's clippers, the bright flower beds weedless. It's obvious to anyone who walks through this section of Berkeley that the Negro families who have moved in take great pride in their property. And it's obvious that they've proved something, for the racial balance in this section has remained relatively constant. The whites aren't running away.

These were the people who used to stop for drinks at the Berkeley Square, white people and black laughing easily together at the bar. Not much, perhaps, to a Harvard sociologist, who never sees such people anyhow. But, given the state of the nation not too many years ago, progress. And I remember just two years ago sitting in a bar in Pittsburgh, a city where racial tensions now are extremely high, drinking Iron City beer and watching a football game on TV. And when the national anthem was played, a half-drunk Slavic-looking construction worker and a half-drunk Negro construction worker put their arms around one another's shoulders and sang "The Star-Spangled Banner."

It's not happening anymore. I visited the Berkeley Square recently, and a couple of young leather-jacketed blacks with their white New Left girls came noisily in

79

and started an argument with the old customers. The old customers left quickly. "Black bastards," I heard the bartender say. He was the same bartender who a few years before had been so popular with Negro customers.

But the Berkeley Square isn't the same now. There are fewer Negro customers. And I suspect that the Negro construction worker no longer drinks with his friend in that Pittsburgh bar.

The New Left and the black militants have done their work well. Older Negroes now live in fear of the tensions created by their militant sons. For although Black Panthers and other such types represent a statistically insignificant number in the black community, they are really the only Negroes (they and the welfare group) whom many sociologists pay attention to. As do the media men. If one were to form one's picture of the black communities only through network discussion and news shows, one would have to believe that they are all gun-toting, looting revolutionaries. Not so, of course, but it's the revolutionaries we see on TV screens. Their parents and older brothers have nowhere to turn. The white establishment will not help, for its leaders are too busy negotiating with the black militants. And the militants call them Uncle Tom or Aunt Jemima and tell them to toe the line or get their heads busted.

Highly visible militants such as Cleaver and Bobby Seale owe their visibility to the university campus—to the New Leftists who have broken the spirits of administrators and reduced them to double-talking appeasers, to faculty who cheer the Cleavers on. Eldridge Cleaver wouldn't have made it without Berkeley. And Berkeley has helped to damage the black community, perhaps permanently.

The New Left has prodded and propagandized, racism has become the national issue, and agitators and militants have insured that the attention of the media is focused on them. As a result America's priorities are seriously out of whack, people are angry, and their anger is misdirected. Race relations, which had been improving slowly but steadily since the late forties, are worse today than at any other time since the first Civil War—thanks to the New Left rag-tailed army and the disproportionate concessions it has won. But despite the sometimes comic-opera, sometimes terroristic antics of fancy-dress strutters like the Black Panthers and other Negro crazies, the vast majority of Negroes fear the militants more deeply than they fear any middle-class white.

The white workingman has been slandered by those who would lay the blame for racial unrest on his shoulders and by so doing rather neatly absolve themselves of any responsibility. He's not a racist. His attitude is not understood by academics who still think of him as one of Marx's proletarians. A man who knows them because he is one of them is Eric Hoffer. And look what has happened to Hoffer's reputation since he came out against the destroyers. They loved him once, since he was a proletarian who also wrote original philosophical works. But he doesn't always use footnotes, he thinks for himself, and, like all original thinkers, he knows what he knows through experience rather than through pleonastic second-hand articles in periodicals. He decided that the liberal academics were wrong, and he is scorned. And in the most small-minded, nastily bigoted way. Part of the problem is his tendency to overspeak, as he did recently when he recommended that college presidents arise daily ready to kill. Liberals are not willing, of course, as in the case of Cleaver, to insist that this is just metaphorical language. And one well-known liberal columnist has even made fun of Hoffer's accent.

But let Hoffer speak: "The simple fact is that the people I have lived and worked with all my life, and who make up about 60% of the population outside the South, have not the least feeling of guilt toward the Negro. The majority of us started to work for a living in our teens, and we have been poor all our lives. Our white skin brought us no privileges and no favors. For more than twenty years I worked in the fields of California with Negroes, and now and then for Negro contractors. On the San Francisco waterfront, where I spent the next twenty years, there are as many black longshoremen as white. My kind of people does not feel that the world owes us anything, or that we owe anybody—white, black or yellow—a damn thing. We believe that the Negro should have every right we have: The right to vote, the right to join any union open to us, the right to live, work, study, and play anywhere he pleases. But he can have no special claims on us, and no valid grievances against us. He has certainly not done our work for us."

But no one will listen to probably the only original American thinker of the past couple of decades. His works make those university types who criticize criticism of criticism sound a bit feeble. But he's non-U. Doesn't have a Ph.D—an M.A.—or even a B.A.! And he *talks* strangely. Who cares if he knows what he's talking about and has something important to tell us? Who cares if he speaks for the white workingman? And the black workingman?

The white workingman has been set against his black fellowman by the abstractionists and the academic theoreticians. Nothing has worked for him. Integrate your schools, he was told, and an age of brotherhood will set in. Reluctantly he accepted the concept of integration. It moved slowly. But it moved. And so the workingman, who traditionally accepts the dicta of those people supposedly more informed than he, accepted integration as a panacea only to discover that everyone still wasn't nice. And now a whole new flip-flop, and he finds himself commanded to atone for the sins of slave traders and Arabs and mercenary African chiefs and embrace something suspiciously like neosegregation and minority-group racism. Keep quiet, he's told, when militants beat his children as they try to buck a picket line of nonstudent Black Panthers in order to get to the classes for which his tax dollar pays.

The new abstraction is white racism. And he'd better believe it or he's a bigot. And he'd better listen to that campus Panther, Eldridge Cleaver, who wants to machine-gun him and his children. And the professors will buy the bullets. And so he's been set against the Negro by those very people he's been taught to respect. But the theorizers know nothing of his life, and to them his role is simply an abstraction. The white workingman has been done a great disservice by the theoreticians, just as the Negro has. Both groups are being pushed into ideological corners, and men who live in the real world fight when cornered. And it won't be just against one another that they will fight.

As professors and administrators are beginning to learn, one can't set a revolution in motion and then retire to the library until it's over.

5

Let me tell you. We manufactured the issues. The Institute for Defense Analyses is nothing at Columbia. Just three professors. And the gym issue is bull. It doesn't mean anything to anybody. I had never been to the gym site before the demonstrations began. I didn't even know how to get there.

—Mark Rudd

Halloween came early to Berkeley. The party was held first at Sproul and then at Moses Hall. The invitations read: "Join us! A sit-in has begun in the Registrar's Office in Sproul Hall. Students from Social Analysis 139X [the catalog designation for Cleaver's course] and other concerned members of the Berkeley community will remain until credit for this course is given or until removed from the building. Although our immediate concern is accreditation for Social Analysis 139X we are aware that our struggle goes deeper than this one particular demand."

Note the wider sense in which the Cleaver issue was meant to be used: "The Regents refused credit for Social Analysis 139X because it represents a direct threat to the racist power structure which they represent [American society]. A militant spokesman for Black liberation [Cleaver] threatens the economic and political interests of the Regents [and the interests of society]. For this reason, the Regents will make every effort to hinder white students' opportunity to participate in an academic endeavor which explicitly makes clear the racism of the University's corporate elite. For weeks, patience and moderation [no violent disruptions, in other words] have ruled. This has gained precious little. The university still contends that Social Analysis 139X has the academic standing of lunch on the terrace. . . . Meanwhile, the Board of Regents discusses not whether to give credit for Social Analysis 139X, but whether to strip the nearly impotent Academic Senate of its last vestiges of power. . . . We ask all who agree that the University is not the servant of Mickey Mouse [this is intended as a funny name for Ronald Reagan, the product of Eldridge Cleaver's devastating literary wit] and Donald Duck [Max Rafferty] to join us in Sproul Hall."

A mild statement, for Berkeley, but it contains all the essentials. The regents are the racists of the corporate elite, the academic equivalent of the military-industrial complex, that bogeyman, beloved by all leftists, that conspires to deprive Americans of their rights. (Funny that the right is sneered at for occasionally believing in a conspiracy, while the left continually indulges in talking about them. Those Kennedy assassination buffs weren't men of the right; nor were those who saw a conspiracy behind the murder of Martin Luther King; nor was Jim Garrison. Obviously conspiracies don't exist, except for rightist ones.) The regents, of course, are symbolic of the men who run society as a whole, Eldridge Cleaver represents the oppressed black man, and the refusal of the regents to allow him to teach a course is an instance of the white racism infecting America.

The party was a great success. Several thousand strangely costumed creatures eventually accepted the invitation. Some capered around bonfires, while others barricaded themselves inside Moses Hall and made merry by scattering professors' files, rifling their desks, and destroying whatever came to hand.

It came as no great surprise to most people at Berkeley—with the possible exception of the professors —that the activists had finally succeeded in occupying a building. They had been yearning to take one ever since their Columbia cousins had upstaged them the previous spring. And running through each noon-hour rally was a wistful attempt to urge students to occupy a building —any building—and get the same sort of media coverage that Columbia had enjoyed.

Up to October, the pleas had not been effective, mainly because none of the issues quite carried the oomph necessary to provoke mass action. But then along came the Cleaver business, and visiting agitators such as Mark Rudd arrived to do their thing. Rudd, traveling the nation on one of those huge but mysterious New Left travel grants, delivered a scornful speech from the Sproul steps. He is a decent-looking kid, although heavy and sluggish, and he speaks in a strangely disjointed grunting mumbling heavy-jawed sort of way. But the message came through.

All the causes that the Berkeleyites had been using, he said, to force confrontations, causes such as academic freedom, university autonomy, students' rights, grapes, simply masked the real issue, an issue, he mumbled, that only the most committed of the Leftists seemed to grasp. The university is rotten and it should be ripped down along with our whole rotten society. This was the message the students had been getting for years, of course, the lesson taught daily by the Marcuses and the Lichtmans, but many understood it for the first time on that day at Berkeley. And so they set out to destroy.

The ostensible reason for their demonstration was still the Cleaver controversy and the whole issue of racism. As Rudd had pointed out, racism was a splendid issue, the sort of abstraction with sufficient elements both emotional and immediate that the quieter liberal academic types could rally round. And so, when the SDSers and other radicals called for direct action, they were careful to do so in the name of racism or academic freedom and free speech, even though they had by this time come to view such causes as window dressing.

The first confrontation, the Sproul Hall sit-in, took place on October 22, when a couple of hundred people, mostly students, occupied the administration building. Most of the demonstrators were students enrolled in the Cleaver course, and when the police finally arrived to cart them off they were reasonably well behaved and the police were courteous. Outside Sproul, however, things were far less civilized. New Leftists, with the help of hundreds of Telegraph Avenue street people and young Negro hooligans, burned whatever was flammable, broke windows, overturned cars, and stoned police. It was a great success, for the apparent idealism of the kids who sat in had won the sympathy of liberal academics, thus insuring that they wouldn't notice the quite different sort of activity that the radicals were engaged in out in the streets. And if they did notice they'd forgive it, feeling the same sort of lachrymose sympathy that they felt for the poor arrested kids. And so the radicals had their excuse for disrupting the campus and forcing the police into a confrontation they were sure no one would want to punish them too severely for.

On the following day it was obvious that they had done their work well. The atmosphere on campus was hysterical and all the causes—the Cleaver course, jobs for Negro professors, grapes—were jumbled into one

emotional casserole. I was sitting in an incredibly boring class in Dwinelle Hall listening to an incredibly boring
talk by an incredibly boring bald young man who spoke
in an incredibly boring mutter, looking up only occasionally in order to shoot great jets of nasal spray into his
nostrils. To this day I have no idea what he was talking
about, but I think it had something to do with computers
and how they'd make our lives so orderly.

His mutterings were completely drowned out by a
group of New Leftists picketing outside, and trying to
block the entrance. I sat by the window, looking out at
the kumquats and the New Leftists. The familiar faces
were there—one a very fat face with a moustache, long
hair hanging over the eyeglasses, and a big swag belly to
set it all off. He was an SDSer whose name I never
learned but who looked a good deal like Humphrey
Pennyworth of the Joe Palooka comic strips. He faithfully attended every New Left meeting and seemed to
fancy himself as a bouncer, for whenever heckling broke
out he'd wander forward menacingly, his thighs rubbing
together inside too tight pants, and frown. Once, at a
meeting in the Berkeley High School auditorium, he not
only looked fierce but also shook his fist. I had long
yearned to let him have one in that obscene hanging gut,
and every now and then, when I'm especially happy and
things are going just right, I vow to go back soon and do
it. Another regular was on the scene, a stumpy, short-
legged, dwarfish type whose great bushy beard and hair
made his head seem as large as a G.I. can, almost as if a
head moved about without a body. Another little bird
who wore a Jerry Colonna moustache was always hopping up on things and waving banners. There was also a
girl, one of the sweethearts of the movement, the same

braless girl I'd noticed the year before, usually closely followed by blacks from West Oakland. Round and round they marched, chanting, "Fuck Ronald Reagan, fuck the regents," over and over again, and it came into the classroom much more clearly than the mumbling lecture we were supposed to be listening to.

I thought about jumping out the window and going home, but decided to do it less dramatically and just walked out, where things were electric. Most of the 27,000 students seemed to be milling around in the plaza. Professors who met their classes droned away to empty rooms about how Shakespeare and Oscar Wilde would feel about Cleaver. The administrators closed down Sproul Hall and went off to drink their lunches. And tourists from Sioux Falls and Ottumwa poured off the Gray Line buses, home movie cameras whirring. On the steps, hysterical New Leftists harangued the hysterical crowds.

No one knew who did it. Perhaps Peter Camejo of the Young Socialist Alliance, a very thin and very intense young man who comes from some obscure place in South America and now lives in Berkeley. His favorite phrase is "this rotten goddamned country," by which he means not the banana republic from which he fled but the United States. He's a striking young man, tall and tubercular lean, and he dresses well and neatly. But most important, Camejo is undoubtedly the finest New Left orator in the country, and when he's on he can move crowds to do almost anything. It's a good voice, middle range and masculine, and his speeches are always extemporaneous, delivered rapidly and with emotion. And when he's good, he works himself up into a fine high rage, and then it happens. If you've ever heard recordings of Hitler's speeches you'll know what I mean. Something seems to take possession of him. The body goes rigid, the eyes blur, then burn, and the voice suddenly kicks into some sort of overdrive, rising a couple of octaves, then locking into automatic pilot, the words racing out, gushing and tumbling, the speaker in the grips of some raging fever, his voice seemingly defying all the natural laws that control breathing. If you agree with such a speaker, you must either act in the way he demands or rush off to get drunk or have a woman. And if you find the ideas of the speaker repulsive, you feel the chills run rapidly through your body and you find yourself gripped by some primitive fear that no amount of sneering or scoffing can alleviate. You want to cry or vomit.

It may have been Camejo or it may have been Humphrey Pennyworth or Jerry Colonna. But someone shouted, "Close down Sproul Hall," and suddenly everyone had taken up the cry and swarmed up the Sproul steps. But the administrators had locked the doors and, although the crowd broke some glass, they couldn't get inside. The New Leftists weren't ready to let the mood subside, however, and so they began to shout, "Close down the chancellor's office," and they raced through the Kumquat Grove back toward Dwinelle, where the chancellor was rumored to spend some time. (I followed, and as I passed the room by the kumquats in which I'd recently been sitting I looked through the window. He was still there, mumbling away, and as he jerked his head up for another shot of nasal spray he didn't seem to notice that there were no students left.)

The activists were unable to reach the chancellor's office, however, probably because they couldn't find it.

Dwinelle is a huge building, as complex as the great pyramids (the rumor is that it was designed by a drunken Egyptian), and the men's room alone is as big as a roller rink. So they shouted "on to Campbell Hall," and everyone then went racing through the kumquats toward the northeastern part of the campus in search of Campbell Hall, the building that houses the computer center. But the university had clearly drawn the line here. No one, not even Eldridge Cleaver, was going to monkey with the computers. The activists had barely enough time to break a few windows before they were routed by police. (A week before, in a rather breaktaking display of contemporary Ludditeism, black militants at the Santa Barbara campus had occupied the computer center and attacked the machines with hammers and wrenches, threatening to destroy the whole works unless their demands—perhaps for printouts in Swahili—were met. They were driven out, however. Nothing on earth is fiercer than a university administrator defending his computers.)

Driven from Campbell Hall, the militants grew noticeably distraught. Poor Humphrey Pennyworth dripped with sweat, and Jerry Colonna got left behind each time he hopped up on something to wave his banner. Thousands of people were running about the campus in thousands of different directions. And many of them were starting to laugh. (New Leftists loathe laughter. One of the Berkeley administration's finest moments came when New Leftists stormed into Vice-Chancellor Earl Cheit's office to present a list of demands. Cheit met them wearing a bright red construction helmet. He called it his "listening to demands hat" and explained that he wore it "to show solidarity with the workers of the world.")

It began to seem more and more like a Mack Sennett chase. The network TV cameramen, most of them portly gentlemen, began to object to running up and down the hilly campus. "On to Moses Hall," shouted the braless girl desperately as she flopped by, closely pursued by her pack of black militants. "Where the hell is Moses Hall?" grumbled a cameraman whose purple shirt had soaked through.

Moses Hall is one of the least obtrusive buildings on the campus and perhaps the smallest. Sandwiched in among several big buildings, it's an imitation Tudor structure, topped by two irregular turrets that were to provide wonderful settings for TV pictures. Jerry Colonna hopped up on one of them to wave his banners, and the braless girl and Humphrey Pennyworth waved red flags from them. (One of the networks sent out for black flags, but none were available.)

Several hundred activists shoved into Moses Hall in the early afternoon, and by evening they had barricaded themselves inside. And things began to quiet down. But as the sun dropped, the street people began to stir along Telegraph, waking from their drug-induced daytime hibernations. They rose from doorways, alleys, lobbies, and from the floors of the small furnished rooms into which they cram by the dozens and sleep in piles, and began to lope toward the campus. Halloween had arrived. They wore odds and ends of uniforms and suits, their hair long and tangled, their eyes red and running, their faces dirty and often mottled with scabs and open sores. They loped onto campus and surrounded Moses Hall, hundreds of them, ripping down fences and whatever else was handy and building huge bonfires, around which they danced and chanted, the chants consisting of four-letter words punctuated by strange animal undulations, a disturbing sound, the kind that Rima, the bird girl, might make on an LSD trip.

Meanwhile, from the roof of Moses Hall, Peter Camejo tried to explain to the crowd just what they were doing and why. "There are only two American Indians on the faculty," he shouted accusingly. But the street people were making too much noise and it obviously wasn't going to be one of Camejo's great days. Before his overdrive kicks in, he has to have the attention of his audience. "We are supporting the struggle of our black brothers," he tried again. (The only Negroes in the building, however, were a parolee from San Quentin and the braless girl's admirers.) Finally he quit and had to settle for posing on a turret and shaking his fist at the cameras.

There are few things I hate more than crowds. I feel that when men crowd together, as they do in New York, for instance, the very lowest common denominator of humanness becomes the daily behavioral standard. And every crowd is a potential mob. Even on the most innocuous occasions. I remember a moment at a Big Ten football game when the officials made a call against the home team at a particularly tense period. The fans erupted, and a long, moaning, semihysterical jeer came pouring out of thousands of throats. I watched a very pretty coed near me as her face twisted and her eyes simmered with hatred, and I honestly believed that it wouldn't have taken a great deal at that moment to send that girl and most of the others in the stadium down onto the field to pull those officials apart and perhaps even to chew on their flesh.

By ten o'clock the continually growing crowd around Moses Hall had become a mob. Students and sightseers and professors with their families and dogs roamed about the campus near the buildings, watching the New Leftists and the street people rip and smash everything nearby and build elaborate barricades across the paths and roads that led to Moses Hall. People waited impatiently for the police, and the screams of the radicals inside the building grew shriller. "We're laying our lives on the line for freedom," they shouted. The street people outside, in the meantime, grew increasingly frenzied as they sucked their reefers, shrieked obscenities, danced around their fires, and threw bricks at windows.

As the scene grew progressively more irrational, as the diseased dancers grew wilder, the academics grew uneasy and strove harder and harder to reduce it all to terms they could understand. It was eerie, frightening, as if one had suddenly been carried back in time to an ancient Celtic heath upon which witches and deformed ogres from the underworld were capering obscenely in the moonlight while others stood by watching quizzically in tweed jacket and necktie.

The professors fought valiantly. One of them—and this is an exact quote—actually said, "They're trying to tell us something." And as a short, fat young man with a face that looked demented and wearing a dress-blue Marine Corps jacket, little green round eyeglasses, and a maroon beret screamed and slavered and smashed on a big piece of construction plywood with a length of sewer pipe, three professors standing nearby looked on and conducted a thoughtful discussion about how to build good barricades. "Why not use some of this scaffolding here?" one of them suggested quietly, pointing with his pipestem to a three-story-high scaffold leaning against South Hall. "Good idea," answered another. "Better start at the top, though." They chuckled dryly. "Fuck Reagan," screamed the street people. "Everyone get bricks," shouted the activists. "We need some goddamn blood," muttered the purple-shirted cameraman.

The bonfires grew larger and as midnight passed the mob began to smash whatever panes of glass remained. Inside Moses Hall the militants emptied faculty desks and destroyed papers. Finally, as the dogs began to copulate around me, I decided to go home. And as I started across the grass I realized that those copulating figures all around the fringes of the mob weren't dogs at all. The street people were properly drugged at last.

Students and faculty began to drift away quickly, suddenly aware, apparently, that what they were watching was actually happening. By the time the police arrived there were only about a hundred left inside and a few hundred outside. One policeman was seriously injured by a brick hurled into his face. One activist was harmed. He had hurt his back building barricades.

And so the Halloween party ended, and the next day the campus seemed to suffer from a collective hangover. People, obviously ashamed of what they had lent themselves to the night before, wore that hangdog look one expects from lynch mobs and wife swappers the day after. Some were even angry. Chancellor Heyns, for one, who must have begun to feel like Neville Chamberlain the day the Nazis moved into Poland, was tuned to a high pitch of moral indignation. The occupation of Moses Hall, he said, was "an act of incredible senselessness," and he declared himself ready to suspend all students involved in the occupation and promised to give full university support to the prosecution of others. He never came through, however.

But not everyone was ashamed or angry, of course. Professor Richard Lichtman, for one, was quite content, and he spent much of the noon rally trying to cheer everyone up. After all, he pointed out, "property is not sacred." Property belongs to people, and people have a right to do what they want to with it (this idea would finally flower completely in the People's Park). Therefore to speak of the occupation of a building as "violence" makes no sense. And anyhow, there are "gradations of violence," he continued. Labor unions once used violence, so why not students? It's our nation that uses violence, he concluded, in Harlem and Vietnam, and the university's treatment of Cleaver constituted "institutional violence." So how can occupying a building and vandalizing be wrong? And a final point: it was all a frame-up anyhow. The police, he said, probably really destroyed those files. (They didn't, it was proved later.)

Forget the logic. Lichtman knew his audience, and his speech had the same effect as a good Bloody Mary. The activists began to believe that they hadn't done so badly after all, and all those liberal professors and students felt a bit better. Within a week the SDSers and their friends were planning strikes and boycotts again. The destroyers had for a day or two seemed morally repulsive to the rest of the campus, but the distaste was dispelled rapidly, and soon the professors were calling again for credit for the Cleaver course.

And so the activists had their occupation and confrontation and their issue. The Board of Regents had absolutely forbidden Cleaver's appointment as a lecturer and had ordered the university not to give credit for it. The militants demanded absolutely that the course be given as planned for credit and that Cleaver be given

99

instructor status. The only concession had been made by the regents, who modified their position sufficiently to allow Cleaver one lecture, despite nearly unanimous statewide opinion among nonacademics that he be prohibited from even stepping on the campus. The regents could go no further, of course, and everyone understood this except the professors. The New Leftists certainly understood it, for theirs was the classic application of the strategy outlined by Ernest Mandel, the Belgian Socialist who had visited Berkeley just before Halloween: "The main strategy for overthrowing neocapitalism in advanced industrial nations today is to put forth, through mass strikes and mass movements, concrete demands and goals which are unacceptable and cannot be granted."

This, plus an emphasis on destruction, redefinition of the concept of violence, plus the issue of racism flavored with antiwar sentiment, plus a good healthy dose of terrorism, plus the new alliance of New Leftists and black militants, plus the unwavering and mindless support of liberal professors who were unable to distinguish between the New Deal and anarchy, plus timid administrators, mixed together and well stirred, was to give the movement its new shape and tactics and make it effective. The last task was to gain the support of large masses of nonideological people, as happened when the Battle of the People's Park erupted in the summer of '69. The radicals had their issues. Now they needed to politicize the masses.

The Moses Hall caper solidified the new alliance, and from that point on the history of the radical movement at Berkeley was the history of the New Left's attempts to broaden its base of support. From Moses Hall on, the campus was never really quiet again. Almost constant disruptions, billed as "student strikes," kept everyone on edge. Cleaver himself suddenly lost his appeal as an issue when his parole was rescinded and he fled to Cuba and then Algeria, sticking his supporters for a huge bag full of bail money.

But Cleaver in person was no longer necessary. Anyone can shout obscenities.

Shortly after Moses Hall, Berkeley was hit hard by the same sort of student strike that had shut down San Francisco State across the bay.

6

They're not like us.

—Jack Kerouac

After Moses Hall, before the student strike, my family and I began in earnest to plan to leave Berkeley. I had known it was all up for me there one day during the summer riots of '68, a day I remember quite vividly. I was enrolled in a summer-session course in which a visiting professor talked about such things as student unrest. He was a most decent man, but the contrast between the civility of his discussions of problems a decade out of date and the periodic sound of explosions and screams from outside made for a horrible incongruity. One tended to feel like a character in one of those tightly structured novels by Flaubert, in which everyone acts on a clearly defined level, each level being distinctly separated from the one beneath it.

I left the class on this July day particularly depressed by a horribly abstract discussion about how best to restructure the university that had ended with everyone agreeing on a structure Clark Kerr had already dreamed up and that obviously wasn't working.

I walked down Telegraph, past a group of street people who had surrounded a tense young Berkeley policeman and were taunting him with obscenities. The windows had been broken in most of the buildings and tear gas was still heavy in the air. A bunch of hard-looking kids walked up to me and demanded some money. "Give us some change, man," one of them said. "Hell, no," I replied. They shouted at my back, and I didn't feel good about it. I turned around then and walked home. Down University Avenue, windows had also been broken. And one that had been smashed out, I saw, was the large plate glass window of Louis Prince, a small, bent old man who collected and sold violins. He was a gentle man and trusting. One day as I passed his shop he gave me a whole handful of checks in stamped envelopes and asked me to mail them for him. He'd never seen me before. On this day he stood near his door, fondling a damaged violin, his eyes wet and bewildered. I got mad, and it all finally snapped into place.

Like the visiting professor, I was a decade out of date. I had come to Berkeley, as I've said, halfway prepared to be sympathetic to the New Left, for I felt that there was indeed a great deal to protest in our land. I'd lived much of my life in one multiversity or another, and I knew that the student too often gets gypped. "Students," said Barnaby Keeney, a former president of Brown, "tend to forget that they have, in a way, 'hired themselves educated,' and that, having hired an institution, they are well advised to abide by the decisions of the institution." This, I had always believed, was pretty much the standard view of most administrators. And it is an offensive view, for there is no provision in it for the student to protest if the institution fails to do the job for which it was hired. You shouldn't have to pay the plumber, after all, if he's unable to unplug your sink.

The typical university student, I believed then and still do believe, is cheated in numerous ways. His fees, usually funneled into graduate programs, buy him lectures not by high-salaried professors, whose services in the multiversity are generally reserved for graduate seminars, but instead by teaching assistants, underpaid graduate students who work one jump ahead of their classes. It's these teaching assistants who provide the slave labor base upon which multiversities build their idealistic programs.

When I had my assistantships at a couple of different universities, I seldom held down less than three jobs at the same time. And this just to scrape by. (Most graduate students with families—and a large percentage have them—are so torturously racked by financial worries that they couldn't do justice to their classes even if they had the time.) And during the same periods, I was drudging along through my own degree program. I found it almost impossible, as did most of the t.a.'s I knew, to do a good thorough job of teaching the undergraduates in my sections. For one thing, there simply wasn't time to work up the material adequately. For another, t.a.'s in general have little practical classroom experience. And then there's the question of subject matter itself. Many large universities seem to use the old army rule of thumb: give the man the job for which he's least suited. I think particularly of my brief stay at Iowa (I left before I was asked to). I'd arrived with good experience in teaching composition and expository writing, general freshman English, and American literature survey courses. My own particular interest at the time was the eighteenth- and nineteenth-century novel. And so I was assigned to teach a couple of strange sophomore-level catchall courses that covered the Bible, Middle English poetry, other poems from my least favorite periods, and a whole bunch of Continental stuff about which I knew absolutely nothing. I did an adequate job, and none of the students complained. And neither did the department head. But it wasn't a good job, certainly nowhere near the job the kids deserved. On many occasions, especially those times when I had a paper due in one of my own classes, I often didn't read the material I was supposed to teach that day until the sun was coming up. And this is the experience of every teaching graduate student I've ever met.

When I was at Iowa, we t.a.'s taught over half the undergraduate courses offered by the university, meaning that a considerable portion of the students there were getting gypped. Of such stuff are comic novels made. And poorly educated undergraduates.

The student is cheated in so many other ways. Those huge upper-division classes, for instance, in which a senior professor reads to several hundred undergraduate and graduate students from old note cards, yellow with age, made thirty years before in graduate school, the same lecture that students have dozed through for decades. At Berkeley, one of the most successful businesses in years pays bright students to go to these lectures and take notes. The notes are typed, photocopied, and sold to other students, who seldom need to go to classes. I bought a set in '68 and took it to classes with me. The professor rarely strayed from the text. Although the notes had been taken semesters before, he repeated them, word for word, even though he trotted out the whole bag of classroom tricks—thoughtful pauses, ironical little apparently off-the-cuff anecdotes, smirks, eye rolling, a cultivated stammer—all intended to give the impression of extemporaneous speaking.

And then there's the young middle-class instructor, determined to break down those middle-class values, who uses the classroom as a forum for advancing his own ideas on the ideal society and consequently distorts any text under discussion to do so. Or the professor who wants desperately to make his lectures "relevant" so the kids will like them. "Sarah Orne Jewett would not, it seems safe to assume, be entirely unsympathetic to to-day's student protests."

The list of academic abuses is endless, and anyone who has ever been cheated out of some chunk of the education he paid for can add to it. And the abuses aren't only professorial abuses. There are also the administrators. There was one at Iowa, the epitome of the contemporary neo-Kafkaesque bureaucrat. An incident remains vivid, the result of the billing process at Iowa. We were living in "married student housing," a little tin shack by the Iowa River complete with a rat that the housing office insisted was a squirrel. Jennifer and Dickie were four and two, and both of them caught pneumonia and had to be treated at the university hospital. And there came one winter month when I found that my $2,000 assistantship couldn't quite stretch to cover those multiple IBM billings. So I took time off from my dishwashing job, to which I went just after I'd taught three undergraduate sections and just before I went to my cooking job, and visited the administration building and explained my situation to a walleyed subordinate subassistant dean who sat there in his tight-bottomed greenish J. C. Penney suit and wrote all the while I told my story.

It was hard for me to do, for I wasn't yet a writer and accustomed to pouring out my troubles to complete strangers. But I plowed ahead, telling my sad story, and when I'd finished he looked up and smiled a funny little smile in his walleyed way and asked me what I had said. And so I did it again, violating a whole code of personal principles, asking a complete stranger to take pity on the plight of my children. And within the hearing of dozens of secretaries. And here's what I begged for: could he arrange to have the billings split up and staggered over the next semester so that I could pay them off without going too deeply into debt? And he leaned back and smiled his walleyed smile again and said of course not. It would screw up the whole billing process. And then he put his head down and started scribbling again and I badly wanted to paste him.

The administrative structure of multiversities often seems the perfect realization of a leftist-collectivist academic dream—completely centralized, intricate and complex chains of command, minute divisions of responsibility, a world of punched cards and forms, where everyone has a number and where everything takes twice as long as necessary to get done. It's always puzzled me that leftist professors seem to dislike their administrations. They've created a system, after all, that is the closest thing on the continent to an Eastern European Marxist state.

My walleyed bureaucrat is not, I think, untypical, and I've made a vow that someday I'll return to Iowa City, tank up on beer at Joe's place, then go over to the administration building. . . .

After seeing those riots, and seeing Louis Prince cry, I knew that I couldn't sympathize with the New Left. The abuses were real enough, which is why the New Left finds recruits readily among students. But to clean up is the job of the reformer. The New Leftists didn't want reform; revolutionaries never welcome reform of the institutions they're trying to overthrow. This is the lesson that college presidents and liberal faculty seem incapable of learning, and they're deeply puzzled when their reforms seem merely to lead to wilder riots.

It's a sad but central fact: there is no room in the multi-versity today for a reformer.

And during the summer of '68, I finally decided that there was no place for me in the multiversity either. So I went home and wrote my first pieces for *National Review*, for writing seemed the only way I could fight. I wanted to tell whoever would listen about what the New Left was up to. It seemed essential to convince people that the New Leftists are no more institutional reformers than the Chinese Communists were agrarian reformers. These kids are revolutionaries, they're smarter than most of us, and when we talk about bringing them into the system they laugh. They don't *want* to be brought into the system; they want to bring that system down. Can you imagine Abbie Hoffman working in a dean's office? This is what liberals cannot believe. And this is why liberals cannot deal with the New Left.

I knew that summer that it was all up for me at Berkeley, as it was for so many others. Classes still met, but they grew increasingly inane and meaningless in view of what was going on outside the classroom. And given the disposition of liberal professors to try to interpret their subjects in terms of current concerns, the classes became increasingly silly. For most professors during 1968–69, it was simply enough to meet classes at all, to make the gesture. They had become victims of the "siege mentality," and each time they succeeded in conducting a class they believed they had done their jobs. The whole idea of *teaching* anything was irrelevant.

I didn't know exactly what I'd do. My articles on Berkeley, I knew, would win few friends *there*. So I decided to get out. To where, I had no idea. But I knew I was a really superb dishwasher.

I'd wanted very much, for a very long time, to live

a life of the mind among scholars in an intellectual community. It was what I had been working toward for the past six or seven years, and an ideal for a good many years before that. But the progress of my education, from the last two years of undergraduate study up through a good deal of graduate, seemed to suggest with increasing emphasis that such a life wasn't possible. And Berkeley proved it. The New Left has made it so, with the active cooperation of those professors who have sold out their profession.

But I had another, even stronger ambition, which was to be able to make my living by writing. It was an ambition I had almost abandoned when I discovered that a growing family couldn't be fed and clothed on those well-structured little short stories that every literature major secretly scribbles away at. So I had decided on a scholarly career. If you can't create it, you can at least preserve it and pass it on, and maybe even help some students to love it as you do.

But this was all over. And then Bill Buckley dropped out of the sky, landed in San Francisco, and asked me to eat dinner with him. So I put on my good graduate school suit and joined him at Trader Vic's, where we drank delicious big filthy brown rum drinks and where he told me he liked my articles and offered me a job as a writer for *National Review*. This was the chance I'd always wanted, the chance to live by writing.

Round and round in circles they marched in front of the main entrance to the campus. Jerry Colonna, Humphrey Pennyworth, the braless girl, a pack of black Berkeley high schoolers close on her tail, and several hundred others. "On strike, close it down," they shouted. "Fuck the regents. Fuck the scabs." Occasionally they'd break into something remarkably like a minstrel show shuffle and chant, "Pow-*ah* to de pee-*pull*," rather as if they'd mastered Negro dialect by studying old Al Jolson records. "We *ah* de pee-pull." Hardly. But they blocked the gate effectively, and at those hours when the traffic was heaviest, they'd link arms, several ranks deep, and prevent nonstriking students from passing. I watched one smallish student who was carrying a slide rule get punched by a beefy hoodlum. I saw a tiny Oriental girl abused by a fat shrieking black woman. And they both came back two days later to be abused as they tried again.

Foolhardy, sure, since there are dozens of other entrances to the campus. But such students wanted to assert their rights. They were registered, tuition-paying students. A good portion of the people who denied them entrance were not. They were absolutely in the right, and the militants had no right whatsoever to block the entrance. But the students received no help. The administration finally ordered them not to use the main entrance and hinted at penalties if they continued to do so. The administrators never ordered the militants to stop their illegal obstruction. And perhaps no other example is necessary to show just who actually holds power on the Berkeley campus.

The occasion was the great student strike. The Moses Hall hangover had worn off, and the militants were more militant than ever. And there were more of them now, attracted by the new issue of black studies, built on the base of the general issue of racism. And so more people were working for the cause now, especially those white liberal professors and students who had been active in the civil rights movement and who had been cautious about getting involved in the previous controversies. But this had appeal. Liberals are great believers in such metaphysical notions as collective guilt. (But I absolutely deny that I should feel any guilt whatsoever. At the time Eldridge Cleaver's ancestors were picking cotton for plantation owners, my ancestors were digging potatoes out of Irish dirt with their fingers and living at the whim of absentee English landowners.) And what better way to purge this guilt than to agitate for autonomous schools of black studies? A good way to give the Negro what we owe him without fouling up our own schools and programs. The point, they say, is to give them pride in their ancestry. (For some reason pride in ancestry is good in Negroes and bad in New England WASPs. And it's strange indeed to watch the same people who fought for total integration in the South in 1958 fighting for total segregation in the academy in 1968.)

The strike had been called by something called the Third World Liberation Front, a group that included the old Afro-American Student Union plus all the Mexicans, Orientals, and American Indians that could be scratched up. (Mexicans and Indians were in short supply at Berkeley, so the radicals bused most of them up from Oakland.) Also, of course, there was a good sprinkling of Black Panthers on hand. The Third World types were joined by the Radical Student Union, a catchall for all the New Left groups, and by the campus locals of the American Federation of Teachers—mostly graduate students at Berkeley.

The demands were essentially the same as the demands made at San Francisco State—an autonomous college in the university, open to Third Worlders, run by Third Worlders. The professors would be Third Worlders and the students would do the hiring and firing. Appointments would be made on the basis of race only, and traditional academic credentials would be ignored completely. The professors naturally got a little tight about this, sensing a precedent that could eventually affect them directly, and the regents, of course, simply wouldn't hear of it. Those few Berkeleyites who still retained some measure of good sense agreed. The university's budget, after all, comes from tax money, and few Californians were willing to finance a school for and by black militants.

Every few days during the winter quarter, Jerry Colonna, Humphrey Pennyworth, the braless girl, and various SDSers and black hoods from Oakland would burst into the classrooms and attack students and professors. On other days they'd hit the student cafeterias and send tables and food flying. And on still other days they'd shout obscenities, smash windows with clubs, throw rocks through the library windows and the windows of lecture rooms. Fires were set all over campus, and on the day the strike was called, Wheeler Hall, the largest and most imposing building on campus, was gutted by a "mysterious" fire, which could be seen against the Berkeley hills from miles away.

One favorite tactic of the strikers, a tactic perfected at San Francisco State, was to hit the library at odd hours, throwing reference books around and emptying cards from the catalog drawers. These card catalogs are monstrous things that fill whole rooms, the work of generations, and they're particularly vulnerable because they sit in the open, unguarded. Without them there's no way in the world of knowing what and where the library's books are. The raids on these catalogs provoked one of the few heroic moments among nonmilitants.

This was the day the SDSers and their black hood allies came dancing toward the library as usual, throwing rocks randomly at windows and screaming encouragement at each other. As they approached the main entrance, an alarm bell shrilled through Doe Library. And when the militants made for the catalogs, obscure little doors flew open and scores of elderly ladies came piling out through them, out of the cataloging rooms, out of the processing rooms, out of the ordering rooms, out of the receiving rooms, out of all those rooms in the building no one had ever seen. They stamped defiantly to the catalogs, scores of them now, ladies who worked out of sight, the ladies who keep any great library running. They put their backs against the drawers and linked arms, their eyes sharp and bright behind bifocals, their sweaters thrown over their shoulders like shawls, their chins thrust out as they faced the militants. The rampagers stopped and shouted obscenities, threatened the women, ordered them to move. They didn't budge, however, and the militants, completely confused, finally left.

But despite such isolated instances of courage, the violence and arson and beatings continued, until even the academics couldn't ignore it. (And this, I think, is an interesting instance of how the liberal mind seems to function. The philosopher for whom the city of Berkeley was named would approve: if you don't perceive it, it doesn't exist. And if it doesn't exist, you obviously don't need to do anything about it. Thus the shrug and the contemptuous lift of the eyebrow when you mention something like crime in the streets. Code words, they say, and this response is perfectly understandable when you finally come to realize that they refuse to perceive the existence of crime. And so, because the word crime denotes something that does not exist, it must mean that you're using the word to designate something else.) But as the winter quarter dragged on, and as the violence increased, they finally had to admit that something bad really was going on. And they demanded that the administration act. (Again it's interesting to note just how bad things—things on the left, of course—have to get before liberals will act. I think, for instance, of the Columbia professor who continually sided with the militants until one of them hit him over the head with a two-by-four, upon which he became a conservative.)

The administration didn't want to take responsibility for the battles that were sure to erupt, however, so it handed the ball to Governor Reagan, who called in the police in force. (Another standard technique of the Berkeley administrators is that when things get so bad they can't control them—and things get that bad precisely because no attempt is made to control them when they're still capable of being controlled—they turn the responsibility over to the governor, who at this stage has no alternative but to send in the troops. When the fighting ends, the administrators then turn around and blame the governor for whatever damage has been done. It worked well up to the People's Park, for Governor Reagan is detested at Berkeley and the people there blame him whenever it rains. And inevitably, just as soon as the community is pacified, the administrators attack Reagan and by so doing curry favor again with their liberal faculty colleagues.)

After several pitched battles the campus quieted down. The strike was broken.

7

Four hours of meetings about tactical matters, politics, and reports from Strike Central. . . . It is announced that we are spending as much money on cigarettes as food. I wonder, as I look about me, whether Lenin was as concerned with the breast size of his revolutionary cohorts as I am.

—James Simon Kunen, *The Strawberry Statement*

In 1968, San Francisco State nearly became the first institution in the country to turn complete authority over to the radicals. Berkeley at this point was like Rome when the men wearing skins rode down from the north and took it over but never completely owned it. San Francisco State was Stalingrad when it seemed inevitable that the defenders momentarily would stop fighting. Then the last of the defenders stepped up to take his stand.

The defender was Dr. S. I. Hayakawa, semanticist and perhaps the most respected figure ever to teach at S.F. State. He is a Japanese-American whose books are used as texts in universities across the nation. In desperation, with nearly their last gasp, the trustees had named him acting president. And then, incredibly, he began to fight back, and the besiegers suddenly found themselves hit by a fierce counterattack. Hayakawa became a national symbol almost overnight, and the militants panicked. The troops disappeared from Berkeley and New Left radicals from all parts of the country landed on the S.F.S. campus. Suddenly there were Humphrey Pennyworth, Jerry Colonna, the braless girl and all her black hood admirers from Oakland picketing across the bay.

Berkeley could wait. The second front had opened, and the radicals were determined not to lose the battle for San Francisco State.

It was a glorious moment, perhaps the most publicized Bay Area event since the earthquake. A band of shrieking grotesques, many of them from Berkeley, milled around a truck parked at the entrance to San Francisco State. Atop the truck New Leftists and black hoods screamed obscenities through sound equipment. "Close it down," they shouted. "Fuck the racist pigs." "Fuck, fuck, fuck," screamed the braless girl, much to the delight of the black hooligans.

Suddenly he appeared among the crowd, just as he had promised he would, and the New Leftists were silent for a moment, unable to believe that he'd actually dare to walk through their ranks. They fell back as he approached, hundreds of them. He walked briskly to the sound truck, a small man, 145 pounds at the most, and sixty-two years old. He climbed up onto the truck, knocked a beefy young militant who tried to interfere with him to the ground, and disconnected the wires of the sound equipment.

He brushed off his hands, good-naturedly shouted back at Humphrey Pennyworth and the other visiting Berkeleyites, then walked briskly through the mob again to his office. And suddenly there was hope, almost as if John Marquand's old hero, Mr. I. A. Moto, had been brought back from the dead once again to straighten out a mess complicated by blundering bubble-headed Yankees. Dr. Samuel Ichiye Hayakawa, the new acting president of San Franciso State, was keeping his promise to do battle with the destroyers.

At first his chances of winning seemed slim indeed, for his only weapon was personal courage, a quality he certainly possesses in abundance. I recall no other president of a besieged college with guts enough to walk alone through a mob of New Left and black militants. And almost daily since the trustees began to consider appointing him president there have been threats on his life and the lives of his family. He has been shot at on at least one occasion, and constantly terrorized, as have those faculty members and administrators who decided to take their stand with him. The home of Professor Edward Duerr, for instance, a Hayakawa supporter, was fire-bombed, the bomb sailing through an open bedroom window. Cars and houses were routinely shot up. Luckily a very minimum of damage has been done. New Leftists aren't very good shots—yet.

The odds seemed heavily against him, for he found himself battling not only the New Leftists, but also most of his own faculty and numerous publicity-hungry black community leaders, like Dr. Carlton B. Goodlett, who can be counted on to come to the support of radicals everywhere. (Goodlett once suggested, "Gun-toting citizens . . . go to campus.") And the Bay Area press was at first curiously hostile. ("They've got themselves hopped up with hostile abstractions about me," Hayakawa said.) And perhaps worst of all, the situation at the college was unusually complex.

The trouble had been building since 1966, when Dr. John Summerskill became president. Summerskill is a strange man, tall and handsome, with a disappointingly reedy little voice. When faced with problems he becomes Hamlet-like. His eyes glaze over and he disappears somewhere inside himself until things get better. There is something remote, distracted, about him.

Summerskill never got off the ground. His inauguration in May, 1967, was disrupted by SDSers, who demanded that the new president stop immediately the practice of giving class ranks to draft boards. Shortly thereafter black militants beat the staff of the student newspaper, sending the editor to the hospital. Summerskill first suspended these black terrorists, but changed his mind when on December 6 militants broke into three buildings, including the administration building, smashed equipment, and promised bigger and better demonstrations unless the blacks were reinstated immediately. Summerskill thought it all over and while he was thinking militants began systematically to tear up S.F.S., instituting a reign of terror that effectively shut down an impressive number of classes. Students were afraid to come on campus.

Summerskill was urged to call the police, but instead he decided officially to shut down the college, an action that enraged the trustees and those faculty and students who believed they had a right to teach and to attend classes. But their rights were ignored, as well as their safety. Summerskill continued to think—and in February decided to resign, effective in September, 1968. The violence continued to increase, however, and in May the trustees asked him to leave immediately. He did so, to accept a job at the national university in Ethiopia (incredibly, shortly after he arrived in Addis Ababa, the Ethiopian university experienced the first student riot in its history).

Dr. Robert Smith, Summerskill's successor, lasted a little more than six months, and probably only that long because no one was quite sure just what he was up to. As riots raged around him, he delivered long nervous speeches, full of educational-school-seminar jargon, "meaningless confrontation," "meaningful dialogue," "relate to one another," a lot of "hopefully's" thrown in,

124

passive and tortured subjunctives. The sort of rhetoric one finds in C— term papers in education courses.

Smith's turn came in September, when a Black Panther and teaching assistant named George Murray stood up on a table in the student cafeteria and urged students to buy guns and bring them on campus. (This advice was followed; the Black Student Union used checks drawn on S.F.S. student funds to buy a semiautomatic Czech rifle and at least thirteen handguns.) Now, this wasn't unique. Men like Cleaver had long been advocating campus shoot-outs. And even former Berkeley Superintendent of Schools Neil V. Sullivan is on record as favoring guns. (He's the man whose work in Prince Edward County, Virginia, resulted in the death of the public school system there, at which point he came to Berkeley and ordered instant integration and then, before the trouble over integration could begin, he resigned to become commissioner of education in Massachusetts. "Many teachers are concerned that ready giving in on the part of the administration to the demands of a small group will convince all students that militancy is the only way to get things done. What is your opinion on this?" he was asked. His answer: "Damn right it is. History has shown that the only way to get things done is get a shotgun and stick it up against the other people's neck." History as interpreted by an educator into whose hands you place the future of your children. And Sullivan's an extremely ambitious man—the rumor is that once he has fixed up Massachusetts like he fixed Virginia and Berkeley, he has his eyes on a Washington Cabinet job.)

So there wasn't anything really unusual about what Murray said. But nevertheless he upset those reactionary old trustees, who, simplistically, found it disturbing that a teacher paid by the state would urge his students to

125

attempt murder. So they ordered President Smith to fire the Panther from his job in the English Department, a department that was and still is the most militant on campus. (Hayakawa blames much of the trouble at S.F.S. on "inflamed literary imagination." During one demonstration Kay Boyle shouted at Hayakawa, "You are a fascist." "Kay Boyle," he shouted back, "you are a fool.")

Smith tried to wriggle out of it, but finally, two months later, he did as ordered. And then the battles began in earnest. The Black Student Union and the Third World Liberation Front called their strike, the terror was stepped up, and, in order to give their cause substance, the militants presented the administration with fifteen "nonnegotiable" demands.

The demands were the same ones made at Berkeley. Demand number three, for instance, commanded that "there be a Department of Black Studies which will grant a Bachelor's Degree in Black Studies." The demand continued, in typically temperate language, that "the Black Studies Department have the sole power to hire and fire without the interference of the racist administration." (Good idea, says one militant Irish-American. His Uncle Sean never went to high school, but he can tell one hell of a good story, especially after a drop of the poteen. A natural as dean of a Department of Irish Studies.) Demand number five asked that "all Black students who wish be admitted."

Nonnegotiable demands, again, and once again the principle stated by Mandel in operation. For the administrators simply can't grant them, even if they are inclined to do so, without breaking laws set down by the California Legislature, and it's the legislature that funds the state college system and pays salaries.

This was the situation that Hayakawa found waiting

126

for him when he stepped onto the stage in November to replace Dr. Smith, who finally, like Summerskill before him, decided to close the college, and who, like Summerskill, was fired by the trustees for doing so. Hayakawa's first action was to open the college for business and to vow to keep it open, no matter what. The militants vowed to shut it down, no matter what. And when they resorted to terror to do so, Hayakawa called in large contingents of police and gave them a free hand to do what they had to do to preserve order, an action that insured the continued operation of the college but won him numerous enemies on the left.

Ranged against Hayakawa on campus were the standard New Leftist groups—the Black Student Union, an organization controlled at S.F.S. by the San Francisco branch of the Black Panthers, the Third World Liberation Front, and hundreds of volunteers from Berkeley and even from as far as New York. But perhaps most dangerous among the opponents ranged against him were some members of his faculty, both those who belonged to the American Federation of Teachers and those committed to radicalizing the college.

San Francisco State had long enjoyed a reputation as a dumping ground for leftist radicals. Dr. William Stanton, for instance, has bounced around from place to place, unable to get hired at California colleges because of his history of radical activities. He was fired at San Jose State because of his leftist proselytizing and, unable to find a job at any other California institution, finally landed at San Francisco State. During the worst periods he walked the picket lines, shouting obscenities at students who tried to attend classes. (He called a garbage collector a "fucking scab," whereupon the garbage man got out of his truck and threatened to poleax him. Stanton

127

scurried over to the police lines, at which he'd been shouting before, and demanded protection.)

The AFT, chapters of which are mushrooming across the country, joined the radical groups in the strike. It's a relatively new organization, formed primarily by radicals and by lower-caste academics. In multiversities the AFT is usually made up of clerical workers and graduate assistants who have M.A. degrees and are teaching part-time while working on Ph.Ds. At colleges that are by definition primarily undergraduate, such as San Francisco State, the AFTers also for the most part tend not to have earned Ph.D.s but, as is the practice in four-year colleges, hold full-time appointments as instructors or assistant professors. They are usually people who lack the credentials—the Ph.D. or significant publication—to get tenure and promotion through traditional academic channels. A man unwilling or unable to earn a Ph.D. and unwilling or unable to do the sort of research that his field considers important has traditionally been expected either to teach at a four-year college or accept a non-tenure post at a multiversity. But the AFT was formed precisely to counteract this, and the demands put forth by AFT locals across the country ask in effect that the old criteria for advancement and tenure be junked in favor of trade union criteria.

For public relations purposes at San Francisco State, however, and to justify to the public their support of the radicals, the AFTers had to come up with some sort of rationale that would make their cause sound something more than merely the angry reactions of a pack of academic trade unionists.

Since Hayakawa was effectively zeroing in on them, with good reason characterizing their attack on the college with the "guns of Singapore" metaphor (the guns of the British defenders were turned outward; the Japanese attack came from inside), a set of formal demands was especially necessary. So they drew them up. Most could be dismissed with a chuckle. They demanded, for instance, better and free parking, surely one of the silliest reasons yet given for actions that led to violence and arson. Most of the other demands were similarly asinine, amply justifying Hayakawa's repeated assertion that the AFTers were simply trying to "ride piggyback" on the student strike in order to satisfy some petty grievances.

There were, however, a couple of demands, set forth over and over again, that many nonacademics thought might be legitimate, demands vaguely explained in the press and on radio and TV by such AFT spokesmen as Gary Hawkins. These demands involved salaries and working hours. They are still being advanced and they tell us a great deal about life in academe.

The demand for better salaries is always couched in emotional vagaries. Salaries at S.F.S., said Hawkins and his comrades, were "30 to 40 percent lower" than at other comparable institutions. First question: what is a "comparable institution"? S.F.S. is primarily a college, its mission to educate undergraduates. True, there's a tiny graduate program leading to the M.A. in a few fields, but this doesn't change the essential nature of the college, since the M.A. today is really an extension of the B.A., much easier to earn, requiring no real expansion of knowledge.

One searches then for comparable colleges similarly set up to provide undergraduate education. And one discovers that S.F.S. pays an average salary equal to that paid by such well-regarded places as Kenyon, Bowdoin, and Grinnell, and the average S.F.S. salary is higher than that paid by Coe, Olivet, Macalester, and

Reed. It's hard to imagine anyone rating S.F.S. higher than these places. It has never been known for much more than its creative writing program. And, speaking of creative writing, we might note that the only other two places with respected creative writing programs west of the Mississippi are the University of Iowa and the University of Denver, a university that pays an average salary $1,000 less than the average S.F.S. salary.

Once a year the American Association of University Professors publishes a complete rundown of salaries paid at all American universities. And their figures, published at the time the S.F.S. AFTers were listing their grievances, show that the S.F.S. average salary was equal to or higher than that paid at *well over half* of our state universities.

Then what *are* these comparable institutions? Must be places such as Amherst, Princeton, and Antioch. Perhaps it's that stuff they're smoking. Or delusions of grandeur. San Francisco is a great city, and its inhabitants are chauvinistic. And some of this chauvinism must have rubbed off on the AFTers. No one with most of his marbles would dream of comparing S.F.S. academically with Amherst or Antioch or Macalester. (Or for that matter Sioux Falls or Yankton College.) Must be, then, that the AFTers have concluded that, since San Francisco is a great city, and since S.F.S. is in it, S.F.S. is a great institution.

The only other justification for higher wages is that, as Hawkins and his friends put it, the cost of living in San Francisco is high. One of them even took to the radio to say that he couldn't buy his children new shoes. This is nonsense. San Francisco is not a great deal more expensive to live in than Denver, Iowa City, and New York (the most expensive place we've ever lived in was Vermillion, South Dakota) if one lives sensibly and doesn't go too often to Trader Vic's for supper.

The question of working hours is similarly a canard. Most AFTers at San Francisco State teach twelve hours per week. If their courses were upper level, and if each time they had to work up unfamiliar material, there could be a legitimate gripe, especially if one objected to working a normal workweek. But courses at a place like S.F.S. are usually elementary and as familiar to the people who teach them as those old shoes they claim they have to wear (and, incidentally, there are some of the finest discount shoe stores in the country in San Francisco). This means that after a man has taught the course a couple of times he really doesn't have to do much preparing, and often there are not even multiple preparations, since the same man is likely to teach several sections of the same class, saying the same things to his eleven o'clock section that he said to the ten o'clock.

And so, what seems on paper like twelve hours' worth of preparation often boils down at most to about six—if the man is conscientious. No matter how he stretches the twelve hours of classroom work plus the necessary hours of preparation time, he still doesn't come out with a workweek much longer than twenty-four hours. Not bad for a nine-month working year at a salary of better than $12,000, the average salary at San Francisco State at the time of the strike. You don't have to be a mathematician to see that this amounts to one hell of an hourly wage. And there are those three summer months, during which he can pick up quite a bit of extra change. There is also the argument that the teachers deserve time off for "research." But it's common knowledge in academe that teachers at four-year liberal arts colleges are hired *solely* to teach. Publish or perish may

131

be the rule at universities. It's *not* at colleges such as S.F.S.

The AFTers represented the soft underbelly of the radical alliance. When I was on the campus, I watched a burly black push a couple of the teachers around. He'd grab their picket signs, then prod them in the tummies with them, chuckling, taunting them with obscenities. The professors tried to play along, of course, as if it were just good fun, but their faces grew crimson as the New Leftists began to crowd around and laugh, and their expressions tightened behind the fake smiles, the same sort of look you see on the face of some poor fat little kid on the school playground as the school bully begins to tease him into a fight and all the little girls gather around to giggle.

As Hayakawa foresaw, it was the faculty strike that collapsed first, and he helped it along by treating the faculty independently of the student militants. People like Professor Stanton were denied tenure and Hayakawa requested that Sacramento cut off the salaries of striking teachers. He stomped up and down the state, heaping ridicule on them, and parents grew increasingly uneasy as they came to realize just what the professors were doing to their children. Before the session ended, most of the strikers were back in the classrooms, fearful of losing their jobs and knowing that they'd have a very tough time indeed finding new ones.

Hayakawa won his war in several ways, the most publicized being attrition. And it's true, of course, that Hayakawa used the police in a way that no other administrator had dared to do. "The innocents who object to police on campus are, it seems to me, profoundly misled by their warm human sympathies, by their imperfect acquaintance with American traditions of law enforcement, and by their inflamed literary imaginations." Mass arrests (nearly five hundred demonstrators on one typical day) plus high bails eventually took their toll. But Hayakawa had no real choice if he was to fulfill his vow to keep the campus open, for San Francisco State was further gone when he took over than any other campus has yet been.

But it was more than just a war of attrition, and there are lessons for administrators in Hayakawa's approach. For one thing, he refused to take a monolithic view of the groups ranged against him. The alliance of New Leftists, black militants, and activist professors, the same coalition that is shaping up on campuses across the country, is not a natural one. The SDSers and other New Leftists are essentially anarchists, their primary goal always to destroy. The blacks are often destructive, but most are sincerely convinced that they're doing the best thing possible to improve the condition of their race. And there are many others who stand with the black militants simply because they have no choice. The discipline of the black groups is fierce, as rigid as that of any Communist party cell, and black students who come to the campus uncommitted find that they either join up and submit to this discipline or get their heads broken—it's well to remember that many of the black militant leaders are killers. But the third group, the radical professors, has an entirely different sort of interest—petty (unlike the New Leftists) and selfish (unlike the blacks).

It is inevitable that partners such as these, bound together by nothing much more substantial than a common hatred, failing to achieve their goals quickly, will begin to squabble among themselves. Black militants have never completely trusted the New Leftists, for they know that, just like the old left, the new views the Negro condition as something to be exploited for its revolutionary value. And they also know that, unlike themselves, most of the New Leftists come from comfortable eastern middle-class homes. When things get too sticky, there's usually a daddy somewhere who'll kick up bail money.

Inevitably, as the cracks in the coalition gaped wider, the strike began to collapse. Hayakawa remained adamant in instituting legal proceedings against those hardcore militants who terrorized the campus, but he spent a great deal of the year wooing the marginal militants, especially those Negroes who stood with the Black Student Union only because they were afraid not to. Most administrators whose campuses have been disrupted have mistakenly accepted the most militant organizations as representative of large groups of students. Hayakawa knew this was not true, that many strikers were strikers out of fear, and he made a point of talking to Negro students individually, guaranteeing them all the protection he could provide. Thus, as the year dragged along, there was a noticeable weakening in the solidarity of the black militants. Terrorism and disruptions continued, but increasingly fewer black students were involved. And it's significant that those picked up in the last campus mass arrest were *all* hardcore militants from San Francisco and Berkeley. For the first time there were no innocent bystanders. And so, by getting tough but not desperately so as the administrators at Berkeley were later to do during the People's Park crisis, by accepting complete responsibility for his actions, and by tempering his toughness with an obvious respect for the rights and the dignity of individual human beings, Hayakawa managed to bring the campus back under reasonable control and to break the siege of San Francisco State. He thus handed the New Left its first major defeat.

Had administrators at Berkeley been willing to act similarly, there would never have been a People's Park crisis and the New Left might well have been left fangless in the capital of their movement. But Hayakawa's lesson was not learned as well as it should have been, perhaps because he is not much loved by either the right or the left in California. Rightists accept his own estimate of himself as a "liberal Democrat," although he told me when I interviewed him one riot-torn afternoon that he may yet end up a conservative. To the leftists, he is public enemy number one. During the worst of the troubles, they circulated handbills throughout the Bay Area urging his assassination.

Hayakawa's fight continues. There are still problems on the S.F.S. campus, and recently Hayakawa accused Dr. Nathan Hare, the self-styled "dean in exile" of the black studies program, of conducting a "reign of terror" by instructing black militants to terrorize pro-Hayakawa professors into resignation. And the future of the college is in doubt because of gift grades handed out to militants by sympathetic professors. This was uncovered recently when the regional accrediting agency visited the campus to renew S.F.S.'s accreditation and discovered that professors had handed out As to striking students who hadn't attended classes.

But it's better than it was. Students now attend classes in relative safety and there are no longer police on the campus. I spent time there during the worst of the battles, had a brick thrown at my head, got a dose of tac squad, watched militants disrupt the library, and got mistaken for a plainclothesman. (And it didn't help the situation when I explained to the pack closing in on me that I was there to do a piece for *National Review*. Fortunately, I'm fast on my feet.)

The troops pulled out, and the New Left retreated to Berkeley to regroup and begin the attack on the university again. In May, 1969, the People's Park battles exploded, and Berkeley has never been the same.

8

You must develop a territorial imperative.

—Eldridge Cleaver

I was in New York when the skirmishes broke out. I called a friend out there whose judgment I trust greatly and he advised me I'd better come out as quickly as I could, for this finally was it, what we'd all been dreading. And so I dropped everything and went back to Berkeley.

It was a beautiful summer day when I landed, and I wanted to cry when I tasted the air again and smelled that strange spicy herblike smell that makes you want to eat the foliage. And makes you wonder why in the world you ever were foolish enough to go back to a tar pit like New York, Bill Buckley or no.

On campus, things at first seemed just as funky as ever. Street people families and stray dogs still roamed among the kumquat trees, several jug bands tooted away, and soon, I knew, at least one girl would begin to shed her clothes. It felt absolutely splendid to be back, someplace again where it was actually possible to walk at a leisurely pace and look at things. I was soft, having been sealed up in the East for a few months, and I was ready, just as I had been when I first came out, to give the dissidents the shadow of the doubt. The news reports had horrified me, and I was prepared to accept their account of the first big battle as an unprovoked attack by brutalized police on mothers and idealistic kids who had made something lovely out of an old pig wallow. But after a few days there, with the blood flowing once more, I knew that I'd been had. Just like the media had been had (as usual), and therefore all those other people who depend on the media for their information about what's going on.

Just beneath the funky atmosphere there was an edginess, an air of hard belligerence. A city police car cruised slowly across the campus (city police had never previously patrolled the campus) and when a Frisbee bounced off the hood and one of the two policemen inside flinched there was a short burst of hard nasty laughter.

Three policemen sauntered, gunslinger style, through the Student Union, pretending interest in bulletin boards and paintings, affecting casual boredom. People fell silent as they passed, and one of the policemen was unable to control a violently twitching nerve in his cheek.

Even during the worst of times, there had always been an innocent unwashed charm about Berkeley. Even during the disruptions—the Sproul sit-ins, the occupation of Moses Hall—there had seemed nearly always to be nearly as much of the comic as the chilling, and although the disruptions became increasingly destructive, most of them were of relatively short duration. But, most important, the great majority of students kept themselves pretty well out of it.

The new mood had been growing, although the comic aspects usually obscured its growth, and the New Left grew along with it. Many people developed the taste during the Stop the Draft Week excesses of 1967. They took to the streets, found that they could disrupt the daily business of a large city, and translated distress with the war into discontent with what they called American imperialism in general. The Moses Hall caper and the whole Cleaver controversy saw a further refinement of issues, with American imperialism being translated domestically into the oppression of Negroes. The Telegraph Avenue riots of '68 were significant mainly because the New Leftists formed a firm activist alliance with the street people of Telegraph Avenue, an alliance that was to prove its value during the People's Park battles. And the winter riots of 1969, ineffective primarily because of the need to send militants to the second front at San Francisco State, were in the end perhaps most important of all, for during the student strike the militant blacks joined the New Leftist-street people alliance.

On May 15, the day the administration tried to reassert control of a piece of university land taken over by the street people, the People's Park battles erupted, and it all crystallized. The Berkeley community became radicalized, and the Oski Dolls (a club for sorority-type chickies) and cheerleaders and faculty wives joined the New Leftists, the street people, and the black militants on the barricades. Pregnant graduate-student wives, editors of the yearbook, members of the interfraternity council marched side by side with the braless girl, Humphrey Pennyworth, and Jerry Colonna, all chanting together, "Fuck the pigs."

After the first battle, *fifteen thousand* students (and they *were* all students) turned out to vote in a special People's Park referendum. More students than had ever before voted for anything at Berkeley—more students, in fact, than had ever attended a graduation, a prom, or a football game—and 85 percent of them voted to

141

oppose the administration's action on the People's Park. And by so doing, they proved, beyond a doubt, that something new has grown up at Berkeley. The radicals there are deeply part of the scene, an accepted part of Bay Area culture. This is not yet completely true of other university communities—Harvard or Columbia, for instance. At Columbia it is still possible for students to mount a somewhat effective opposition, as the Conservative Student Union did during the latest troubles. True, they were nowhere nearly as effective as the New Leftists, but they did at least represent a visible opposition, a recognizable cultural alternative.

At Berkeley there are no real alternatives left. The radical groups are absolutely central. And they operate in a society that has no objective correlative in the American experience. For what has grown up there is a completely alien culture. Its values are not ours, its mores are unique, its life-style unclassifiable in whatever terms are available to us. And it is spreading, as witness the recent rash of rock festivals at which thousands of youngsters have appeared on the East Coast, not yet political but well on their way to becoming full-fledged citizens of the new society. They are not yet New Leftists, but they have taken the first giant step, and the New Left is there waiting for them. This is the way it began at Berkeley. First the process of socializing, then the politicizing, which comes easily once the social mores of the culture have been accepted.

Most of the radicals came to Berkeley not too different from students anywhere. But over a period of time their frames of reference began slowly to slide, their values being eroded subtly, bit by bit. Anyone who has done time at Berkeley knows how it works. It even happened to me, and I'm the only right-winger I ever met there. At first there's the cultural shock. Everything —the buildings, the foliage, the people—is different from any other place in the country. But at the end of a couple of months it looks normal. And after a year or two you feel that Telegraph Avenue is like any other main street in the country.

This is the first part of the process. Once the scene seems normal, it becomes very easy to accept other bits of the culture. Rock music suddenly seems not at all jarring. And everyone knows that university administrators are second-rate jackasses, so isn't it all to the good that the SDSers keep them on their toes? And what kind of bastards would cause all that trouble over something like the People's Park? After all, the park people were doing something constructive, weren't they? And there's really something kind of humane about that Telegraph communal life, isn't there?

The professed intent of the New Left has long been to radicalize and organize the young ("We're going to steal your kids"), to urge them on toward the destruction of the institutions of our society. A farfetched notion, of course, and one that the rest of the country is inclined to scoff at. We'll muddle through, they think. After all, haven't we always? But if People's Park proves anything, it proves that the ideal is no longer quite as farfetched as it once seemed. Each year Berkeley swallows a new crop of high schoolers, and increasingly the more attractive and intelligent among them either help to people the street culture or, at the very least, feel comfortable in it. It begins much earlier now. Berkeley High School is, if anything, even more radicalized than the university. And this is becoming true across the country. Read those daily papers carefully and notice how often high schools are closed down by raging militants. Even in Fairfield, Connecticut, as straight and untouched a place as exists within reach of New York, the SDS has infiltrated the high schools and publishes an obscene and revolutionary student paper. As the radicals get younger, the once clearly defined boundaries that separated this alien culture from the traditional culture become less and less distinct. The Berkeley pompon girls may not soon take to the streets, much to the disappointment of male militants, but they are no longer uncomfortable with the radical street culture, and have come to accept it as not only an authentic one but, most dangerously, a normal one. When the radicals marched on People's Park, they led a great pack of ordinary students who didn't question the desirability of direct militant action in the name of communal property.

The People's Park battles were by far the greatest confrontations yet to hit an American university and its community, dwarfing the uprisings at such places as Columbia and Harvard and Cornell, which ripped up institutions but did not take entire cities with them. For in Berkeley today there is a residue of radical bitterness thicker than that at any other campus.

Not only were more people involved, but the nature of the conflicts—more like full-fledged guerrilla warfare than the campus riots to which we've become so dangerously accustomed—set a precedent. There was the now famous helicopter gassing, catching hundreds of students. A good friend found himself caught in Sproul Hall. He, along with the dean of the graduate school and several university officials, members of the student discipline committee, were in a room debating, ironically enough, just how tough a line to take with student militants. Gas came suddenly billowing through the open windows and they raced outside, choking. But as they

144

paused on the Sproul steps to try to gasp in some air, a policeman lobbed a canister of tear gas at them. It exploded at their feet. Another friend, working in the library, hit the deck when bullets began to spatter against the walls. He showed me the bullet holes near the humanities graduate reading room. I put my fingers in them. Real bullets, baby.

The scenes would have been thought impossible a few years ago. James Rector, his insides torn by buckshot, fatally wounded, his blood running down the shingles of a rooftop. Another man, permanently blinded. A policeman taking deliberate aim at a fleeing Berkeleyite's back. Other policemen grappling obscenely with hysterical girls. (And the hardest right-wingers among us can't deny that many policemen went berserk.) Other scenes: National Guard bayonets creasing the stomachs of spectators caught in military flanking movements; troops bivouacked in downtown Berkeley, a scene straight from Europe, cooking fires gleaming among stacked rifles.

Any account of the war of the People's Park must consider four basic questions: who, what, how, and why? First the what and how. Thus far there have been three major accounts. One, by Berkeley professors Wolin and Schaar, both liberal-leftists and both consistent apologists for militant activities, appeared in the *New York Review of Books.* Another has been printed in *Ramparts,* and a third is a detailed report compiled by Governor Reagan's staff. (A fourth has recently been issued by the Alameda County supervisors, but it covers no new ground.)

The Wolin-Schaar piece is least revealing, for the professors have an ax to grind: they want Reagan and the administration to take full blame and to emerge as the

145

only real villains. As a result, most of the analysis is distorted, often inaccurate. Although it's a long piece, it is general and evasive, and one suspects that the authors wrote it primarily to expound, as they could do at the end of the piece with great relish, on the nature of bureaucracy. And ironically, as a result, they end by doing exactly what they accuse the bureaucrats of doing—"the bureaucratic mode of knowing and behaving comes to constitute the things known and done themselves," they say. Precisely. Wolin and Schaar translate the whole conflict into the abstract world of high academe, where today's riots become just about as immediate as the agitations of the Anti-Corn Law League. They set up imaginary chains of causality, impose order on the disorderly and pattern on the patternless, make the irrational rational; and the academic method, like the bureaucratic method they criticize, becomes the thing itself, from which self-created thing they then proceed to draw tautological conclusions.

The *Ramparts* and Reagan reports are much more useful in establishing the whats and hows. The whats are these. The People's Park is a 270-by-450-foot piece of land, about five blocks deep inside Telegraph Avenue street people territory on the 2400 block, the favorite gathering place of drifters, militants, dope pushers, Hell's Angels. It's perhaps the toughest section in the whole Bay Area, and the street people control it. Police are reluctant to patrol this area, and on those occasions when they attempt to make arrests for such things as narcotics violations or rape, they are attacked by the crowds.

At one time there were old houses on the People's Park site, but when the university bought the land in June, 1967, these buildings were demolished. The Board of Regents had authorized the purchase with the proviso

146

that the land be used for sports playing fields, but it wasn't until 1969 that there were funds available to begin laying them out. And during these two years the plot grew increasingly unattractive, littered with debris left from the demolition of the buildings. People began to dump trash there, and students used it for a parking lot or a place to ditch broken-down cars. The university administration did nothing, and as the lot came to look more and more like a pig wallow, many people in the community began to complain. And so, when an apparently nonpolitical group of people took it upon themselves to clean it up, few Berkeleyites were upset.

But here things get cloudy. According to Chancellor Heyns, the university had begun in March to draw up plans for the fields to be laid out on the site, a month before the work on the People's Park began. Not so, say the park's builders. The university, they claim, didn't dream of developing the property until after the people began their project. The people themselves, say the *Ramparts* writers, were not New Leftists or even predominantly street people, but Berkeley residents—students, mothers, children—and the militants had no hand in bringing about the confrontation. The fault lies solely with a bumbling, callous university administration that panicked and played into the hands of the evil man in Sacramento. The Reagan report denies this. The whole thing was a carefully planned confrontation engineered by New Leftists. The truth seems to lie a little in between. Thousands of innocents were sucked into the battles, as *Ramparts* claims. But there is ample evidence to support the contention of the governor's office that the militants had purposely worked to bring on the confrontation.

On March 31, the Telegraph Avenue edition of the

147

radical *San Francisco Express Times* suggested that militants use the site for a park. And on April 20, a month after the administration claims to have made firm plans for developing the property, the voice of the Bay Area underground, the *Berkeley Barb,* called for the occupation of the lot:

> A park will be built this Sunday between Dwight and Haste.
> The land is owned by the university which tore down a lot of beautiful houses to build a swamp.
> The land is now used as a free parking space. In a year the university will build a cement type expensive parking lot which will fiercely compete with the other lots for the allegiance of Berkeley's Buicks.
> On Sunday, we will stop this shit. Bring shovels, hoses, chains, grass, paints, flowers, trees, bulldozers, top soil, colorful smiles, laughter and lots of sweat.
> At one o'clock our rural reclamation project for Telegraph Avenue commences in the expectation of beauty.
> We want the park to be a cultural, political, freak out and rap Center for the Western world.
> All artists should show up and make the park their magical possession. Many colored towers of imagination will rise above the Forum and outdoor Telegraph restaurant and into the future of reality. Pastel intertwining the trees and reflecting the sun, all Berkeley energy exploding on the disappearing swamp. The University has no right to create ugliness as a way of life. We will show up on Sunday and we will clear one third of the lot and do with it whatever our fantasy pleases. We could have a child care clinic or a crafts commune. . . .
> This summer we will not be fucked over by the pigs "move-on" fascism, we will police our own park and not allow its occupation by imperial power.

All the elements are there: aesthetic appeals to those liberals ready to be sympathetic to anything smacking of conservationist concerns, and for the militants contempt for property, communal ownership, domestic imperialism, the university as the symbol of the national government. Other organized radical groups also agreed on the potential value of the park as a "cultural, political, freak out and rap Center," and May was devoted to codifying the ideology and translating the coming confrontation into New Left terms. "Earl (Bull) Cheit is full of it if he thinks he is going to bulldoze a blade of grass in the People's Park," wrote Stew Albert in the *Barb* shortly after hundreds of people, many of them good-hearted liberals who saw the whole thing as a nice Arbor Day type of project, turned out to clean up the lot. "The Pentagon Pigs thought Vietnam would be an instant parking lot for their Army of Atomic Cadillacs and now are afraid to land a quivering helicopter on Saigon." Thus the People's Park issue is neatly equated with the war in Vietnam.

"The concept of property is also important here." Albert continues, " 'You must develop a territorial imperative,' Eldridge Cleaver once rapped to the Berkeley Left. He believed the only way we were going to get serious about Revolution was when we had something in the soil to defend. We have it—the People's Park and its avenging angels are everywhere." Steve Haines, another *Barb* writer, seconds this notion: "The idea that the people can take an ugly barren lot and convert it into something useful and beautiful strikes at the very heart of capitalistic concepts of private property." A leaflet issued during this period spelled it out further: The People's Park project was the first important stage in the war between the "Industrial-University Machine and our Revolutionary Culture. We need the park to live and grow and eventually we need all of Berkeley. . . . If the

University attempts to reclaim $1.3 million worth of land now claimed by the people, we will destroy $5 million worth of University property."

Clearly the militants saw in the People's Park the chance to take property, which they would then govern themselves, preparation for that revolution they're determined to bring on. And they expected support, for what better issue to arouse the community than green grass and pretty young mothers over against parking lots and soccer fields? The Berkeleyites swallowed it, and up until May 15 there were at least as many nonpolitical types working on the park as there were militants. Didn't they know they were playing right into the waiting hands of the New Leftists? Of course they did, in a way, for all Berkeleyites know what the radicals intend at any given time. Everyone reads the *Barb,* picks up the handbills, listens to the rally speakers. But at the same time, although they knew what was going on, they also had no idea of what it would lead to. This is a result of the peculiar way in which facts simply roll off the liberal consciousness. Let militants stage a destructive confrontation and the academic community is horrified; two weeks later, however, they're all saying once again that it's the fault of the war in Vietnam, white racism, and the industrial-military complex.

The liberal consciousness remains peculiarly selective. "We need the park to live and grow," say the radicals. You're right, answer the liberals, and isn't it nice. "And eventually we need all of Berkeley," the radicals continue. Why, that's just hyperbole, respond the liberals, even though it's part of the same sentence and represents a logical progression. (David Hilliard, Black Panther leader, announces at a Moratorium demonstration at Golden Gate Park that the Panthers will kill Richard

Nixon. Just symbolic language. The Panthers publish in their newspaper detailed blueprints that teach kids how to make bombs out of aerosol cans. No one notices.) "At one o'clock our rural reclamation project for Telegraph Avenue commences in the expectation of beauty." Beauty and reclamation projects are *so* nice. "This summer we will not be fucked over by the pigs 'move-on' fascism, we will police our own park and not allow its occupation by imperial power." They don't really mean *that*. And anyhow, the poor children have some right to be upset over this imperialism business. And here too, of course, another hint about why the People's Park was so startlingly effective. For the whole notion of private property has been one of the favorite butts in liberal classrooms across the country. ("Notice, chuckle-chuckle, it does *not* say 'life, liberty, and *property*.' " One famous professor made his reputation by insisting that the writers of our Constitution were property owners and thus suspect, and Professor Richard Lichtman points out that there's nothing morally wrong with ripping up property.)

There is an attitude that underlies the dogma of contemporary liberalism. It's not always spelled out, but it's the tone of voice, the lift of an eyebrow, that little ironical smirk, that dry little chuckle, whenever something like "middle-class morality," "religious values," "Barry Goldwater," "Republican" is mentioned. And thus with the notion of "private property," a concept somehow vaguely shameful, just like "the self-made man" or "rugged individualism." You spend a few years in the academy and even though you may be the staunchest of conservatives you find yourself feeling uneasy when you hear such terms. So when the university administration tried to justify its actions in the People's Park confrontation by arguing that it owned the land and had the legal right to do anything it wanted to with it, good indoctrinated liberals hooted and jeered. And in the meantime, they wholeheartedly pitched in to help the militants build their park and prepare for confrontation. Their contempt for the whole notion of property left their consciences clear and they expropriated the university's land; their way of viewing the world selectively allowed them not to perceive what the radicals who used them were up to.

No one paid much attention to the May 9 manifesto, which began: "We take a solemn oath to wage a war against the University if it begins to move against the park." And when Art Goldberg wrote proudly that the park was "the Beginning of resistance," everyone just shrugged. Even when he added that the People's Park was launched "by five or ten old-time politicos" and was "a calculated political effort" rather than "a spontaneous joyous outpouring," no one paid any attention. No one seemed willing to read the colored poster handed to any Berkeleyite able to walk: "We are building a park on the land. We will take care of it and guard it. . . . When the university comes with its land title we will tell them: 'Your land title is covered with blood. We won't touch it. Your people ripped off the land from the Indians long ago. If you want it back now, you'll have to fight for it.' "

A few people heard and understood, of course. One was Berkeley City Councilman John K. De Bonis, who, in a letter to the regents dated a week before the battles began, charged that the park was "conceived and is being directed by a clandestine revolutionary group specifically to precipitate a major confrontation with the police and the university administration." Subsequent investigations have borne out De Bonis's statement. Among those responsible for the planning of the park: Michael Delacour, one of the Moses Hall leaders; Stewart Albert, arrested in Chicago during the convention disturbances and also a Moses Hall leader; Paul Glusman, another Moses Hall veteran; Frank Bardacke, William Miller, Michael Smith, and Reese Erlich, all veterans of on- and off-campus riots and longtime New Left leaders. And dozens of others, most of them prominent in Stop the Draft Week, the Telegraph riots, and the seizure of Moses Hall. But few listened to De Bonis. He's a conservative.

And so the work continued. and the community pitched in. But those people who did hear De Bonis began to grow nervous, among them Chancellor Heyns, who was one of the few, to his credit, who understood what was going on. "We've got the perfect issue," he said, quoting the militants. "The people versus the heartless university. . . ." Heyns had begun to get hit with flak from both sides. On the one hand, a small but growing band of vocal Berkeleyites circulated petitions demanding that the university take charge of its property. Berkeley is still primarily a residential city, and many of the people who live there own homes bordering on the steadily spreading street people territory. In the past few years, these people, many of them elderly, have watched their once lovely city become one of the highest crime areas in the country, and most of them today fear to leave their homes after the sun goes down. They have lived through destructive riots (the '68 Telegraph riots cost a quarter of a million dollars in property damage alone, and this is only part of the total when one takes into consideration the costs of increased tax rates and deteriorating property values) that were staged on and launched from the university campus, and they believed (and the militants agreed) that the People's Park would provide a second sanctuary and staging area deep in the heart of the street people's territory.

And from the other side came pressure from the militants themselves, openly aiming to provoke the biggest confrontation yet seen. "It was obvious to us the nature of our response was very important," said Heyns's spokesman, Earl Cheit, after the first big battle. "It was the big stupid university responding to something gentle. We tried to respond with reason, and we also wanted to respond to the needs of students and people in the area. It was clear reason and discussion would not work and there was also a growing attitude that this was their land, that more and more people were involved. We realized that if we waited the confrontation would be much larger."

The "reason and discussion" that Cheit mentions refers to a series of emergency meetings between Heyns and the radicals, meetings that Heyns described to the Academic Senate late in May: "The anonymous developers could not form a responsible group with which we could deal. The representatives . . . refused to accept the basic premise: that the design and use of the area was finally the responsibility of the university, no matter how flexible the design or how liberal the use." Of course the militants wouldn't accept the basic premise. Nothing is more touching than a rational administrator attempting to impose reason on the irrational. The radicals were later to mock Heyns for his belief in negotiations. They had nothing to negotiate except the terms of surrender. "The attitude of people working in the park was becoming increasingly belligerent," Heyns continued, "and the development was proceeding on a scale which heightened the danger that if the university did not assert its owner-ship soon, a massive confrontation might result."

And so, on May 13, Heyns took his stand. "It is now clear," he said, "that no one can speak for the anonymous developers and no one can control the grow-ing safety, health, and liability problems in the area." He then announced that the university would put up a fence around the park so that it could be surveyed and pre-pared for development, and in a final attempt to be reasonable he offered to allow part of the site to be devel-oped as a park. The street people would have none of it. On May 14, university police nailed up fifty-one No Trespassing signs around the park and early the next morning police surrounded the site and ordered everyone off. A construction crew and nearly three hundred offi-cers from the Berkeley Police Department, the Alameda County Sheriff's Office, and the California Highway Pa-trol were on hand when the sun rose. But there was no attempt to interfere with the crew and by noon of May 15 most of the police had left.

The scene at the park site was peaceful. On campus, however, several thousand Berkeleyites were milling around. The noon rally featured nine speakers. The sub-ject was the People's Park. Michael Lerner, the disciple of Professor Richard Lichtman, set the tone: "If the idea of people deciding what to do with their own lives catches on, it will bring down capitalism and the establishment can't stand that."

The crowd roared. And then Dan Siegal, the student body president-elect, stepped to the microphones. ". . . If we are to win this thing," the university police's tapes have him saying, "it is because we are making it more costly for the university to put up its fence than it is for

155

them to take down their fence. What we have to do, then, is maximize the cost to them, minimize the cost to us. So what that means is people be careful. Don't let those pigs beat the shit out of you, don't let yourselves get arrested on felonies. . . ." And then Siegal shouted, "Let's go down and take over the park." (Later, on trial for inciting to riot, Siegal claimed that he had meant to say more, to *calm* the mob. Of course, he had just finished working them up. He was acquitted.)

They marched, several thousand of them, radicals, nonradicals, side by side, down Telegraph Avenue chanting: "Take the park. We want the park." As the mob moved down Telegraph the police, badly outnumbered, were caught unawares. Seventy-five policemen threw up a hasty skirmish line half a block from the park, and a small group of Berkeley police and California highway patrolmen blocked the Haste Street entrance. As the crowd came on, it began to chant, "Fuck the pigs," and the activists among the marchers began to throw rocks and bottles, smashing the windows of stores and cars.

(The poor old Bank of America, which in 1968 had been remodeled, had its large handsome windows smashed once more. The last time I visited Berkeley, the windows had been bricked up. It looks like a fortified Guadalcanal pillbox. I *know* it's hard to feel sorry for anything as big and rich as the Bank of America. One can't quite feel for a corporate giant in the same way one feels for Louis Prince, the violin maker. But in defense of the Bank of America, whose windows are routinely broken during every new riot, I've never known a banking institution kinder to students. Any Berkeley student who is officially enrolled can walk in off the street and pick up a loan with a minimum of red tape and waiting. I did it when I first arrived, broke and with

156

no credit rating whatsoever, pursued by half the collection agencies in the Midwest.)

The crowd split into two groups, a couple thousand moving down an alley that led directly to the park, the others moving west along Haste Street, attempting to surround the officers. People on the rooftops threw rocks, bricks, steel pipes, and homemade bombs on the police, some of whom began to fall from direct hits and from crowd pressure. As the fighting intensified, the police tried to single out the more violent activists from the mob but, squeezed in by the closing circle of screaming protesters, they were increasingly unable to determine who was attacking and who was being pushed. Finally, as small groups of police were surrounded and beaten, sheriff's deputies began firing tear gas canisters. Some of the nonmilitant demonstrators tried to disperse, but they were wedged in and pushed forward by the New Leftists, who directed the charge from the outer fringes of the crowd. As policemen continued to fall, the commander of the Alameda County sheriff's contingent decided that the situation was desperate. The deputies fought their way with clubs back to the campus and were issued shotguns, then fought their way back down Telegraph to attempt to rescue the California Highway Patrol officers, who, although surrounded and badly mauled, refused to draw their pistols at any time during the riots. As the deputies moved in they were showered with barrages from the rooftops. They responded with blasts from their shotguns. It was sometime during this period, about 2 P.M., that James Rector, one of the people on the rooftops, was felled by a shotgun blast. Rector died the following night.

It's important to note that the deputies are not, for the most part, men with any real expertise in law enforcement. This is a part-time business for them, and many, according to a friend who has watched and listened to them carefully, make no bones about loathing the Berkeley activists. There is no doubt that they reacted too violently, that they should never have been given shotguns, and that they should never have fired. While Rector's record strongly suggests that he was more than an innocent bystander—he was on probation and had been arrested for charges ranging from grand theft to narcotics violations—no one had the right to kill him. And the fact remains that many of those injured by shotgun pellets were indeed innocents who had been sucked into the riot by the militants.

I hold no brief for such actions, and I think that had I accidentally been swept along by the mob and had I seen a deputy shooting into the crowd, I would have taken a poke at him. I certainly would have tried to identify him later. But I think I would also have done my best to help those highway patrolmen, perhaps, incidentally, the most impressive state law enforcement body in the country, who were trapped but refused to use their weapons for fear of harming people not really responsible for their actions. And one must also say in defense of the deputies that, given their lack of police expertise, they did the best they could to control the crowd and rescue the trapped patrolmen. The deputies, after all, were caught up in a mob that had lost all control, a mob that had become a primitive, screaming, atavistic, milling gang, suddenly tasting blood and yearning for more, a mob that had lost everything human in a great whirlpool of barbaric emotionalism, a mob that singled the deputies out as the enemy, clubs versus steel pipes and bricks, and outnumbered twenty to one.

As for the argument that they shouldn't have been

there at all, their presence was not voluntary. The university officials had requested massive police protection, which was generously supplied. But the Bay Area police have duties in their own communities, and in order to flesh out the force sent to the university, the Alameda County officials had to send the deputies, the only group of sufficient size that could be spared. And so, in the end, although as individuals the deputies who overreacted must be held responsible as individuals, the people who were responsible for their being there must accept a large share of the guilt for the wounding of innocents and the killing of Rector. Chief among these people were the university administrators who had let their control of their campus, through years of appeasement and timidity, deteriorate to the point where such police action was necessary.

The administrators weren't about to accept any blame, however. President Hitch said, "I deeply regret that those in authority decided that certain tactics were necessary to protect persons and property, but these and other tactics are not the responsibility of university authorities." Hitch then went on to lay the responsibility at the feet of the city manager for calling in the troops and at the feet of the sheriff of Alameda County for misusing them. (Later, the administrators were to lay all the blame for the National Guard at the feet of Reagan.) This pleased neither the sheriff nor the city manager, who insisted that Chancellor Heyns had indeed asked for police assistance. But he also had asked the city manager to do it for him. Heyns similarly shrugged off any responsibility. ". . . How they [the police] were used is not my responsibility," he said dishonestly, for anything that involves his campus is his responsibility. But it's the old reflex, the Berkeley administrator keeping his career alive by evasion. (Thus, as previously, anytime a mob organized on campus to attack surrounding communities, the administrators with great piety denied having anything to do with it, even though they had usually allowed the militants to use university facilities as a staging area.) At the end of his statement, as if to prove that the real world has nothing to do with academe, at a time when wisps of tear gas still wafted through Berkeley buildings, when troops occupied the city, Heyns concluded with this rather astounding sentence: "We haven't stopped the rational process."

And, of course, the radicals simply mustn't be let off the hook. They started it in the first place, and it was their actions that brought in the police and, eventually, the National Guard. This seems obvious: people rioted, the police tried to control them, since one obviously doesn't want rioting people taking over a city. And later, when the rioting continued and the university completely lost control over the students placed in its charge, the governor was asked for assistance and sent in the troops, this being the only form of assistance he could possibly give to the riot-torn campus and community. First riots, then troops. No riots, no troops. But on the twenty-first, six days after the worst of the rioting, and during a period when the city and campus were still being terrorized, Governor Reagan was visited by a delegation of professors who demanded that the Guard be withdrawn. The spokesmen were Professor Owen Chamberlain and Dr. Leon Wofsy. "You've created the atmosphere of violence on campus," Wofsy shouted at Reagan. The presence of police and guardsmen on campus was responsible for the violence, added Chamberlain. This is the sort of thing that drives the governor and all conservatives up the wall. "We did not put the police and the National Guard on campus first and then find that trouble followed," Reagan said carefully, trying desperately to explain the obvious. "Are you telling me that the radical group, the revolutionaries, the rioters who started this . . . if we remove the police and the National Guard, they will give up these storm trooper, Hitler-like tactics and go ahead with their education as they should?" This made no sense to the professors. The revolutionaries, responded Chamberlain, humming that same old dismal tune, are a "very small group." "We must take a new and different direction," said Professor Wofsy, whose direction has always been hard left. "We seem to be getting down to who started the war," answered Reagan. But this wasn't the case, of course, and the professors left the governor's office and returned to Berkeley to preach the illogical gospel.

Somehow, within a few days, everyone at Berkeley forgot that the police had initially acted only after being attacked. As the legend grew, nearly everyone shortly came to believe that innocent students and their young families had just been going about their daily business when they were set upon by bloodthirsty policemen sent by a governor who had decided that genocide was the only answer to the Berkeley problem. Forgotten was the careful preparation for action by the New Leftists and that charge down Telegraph Avenue on the fifteenth. "Stop Police Terror!" shouted one typical New Left leaflet. "Yesterday the police shot students and members of the community, blinding one, collapsing the lung of another and wounding sixty more. The attack was carefully planned. The National Guard had been alerted, helicopters were on hand, special weapons were deployed, and hundreds of police specially mobilized. This could only have been a premeditated attack! Using the park as an excuse, those who control this society are attempting to terrorize students in an effort to prevent them from building a nationwide movement against racism and imperialism." The attackers thus become the attacked and the student movement part of a much larger war against the whole system. Thus have leftists, both old and new, rewritten history for decades.

Then came the ideologization, the casting of events into the proper party line form, pitched at those innocent liberals who were still not quite sure what had happened but were willing, as usual, to accept any explanation that appealed to their conditioned reflexes. "Yesterday's violence was minimal compared to what the people in the ghettos and Vietnam face every day. But it made it clear that the people in power are depending on nationwide repression to stop students fighting for progressive change," from another handout. Thus, the People's Park becomes a miniature ghetto and a miniature Vietnam, the university and the governor become the federal government, their repression aimed at students who, in the People's Park, were merely, like their black brothers and the Vietcong, working for progressive change. "Berkeley is not an isolated phenomenon. Last month at Harvard pigs brutally attacked students who were fighting to smash ROTC and stop university expansion." Violence on the part of activists is not violence at all, of course, when they exercise it to smash ROTC and disrupt the university. Only the "pigs" exercise violence, a la Lichtman and Marcuse. And most good liberals agree.

"We must not be intimidated! The increasingly antiracist, anti-imperialist character of the student movement has scared those who have a stake in the status quo [the status quo being, of course, the American system]. Increasingly unable to fool students, they have to rely on

162

sheer force to protect their interests. The only way to defeat this force is through mass militant action." And so the People's Park confrontation becomes something it was not. "For the last month everyone from the NY Times to Attorney General Mitchell has been calling for a stop to student rebellions by whatever means necessary." And within a week most liberals, ready to believe almost anything short of Satanism of the Nixon administration, saw the whole thing as a government plot.

The radicals were careful to pitch their arguments to the liberals in a way that would play on the heartstrings and stir up the sludgy mindless sentimentality that characterizes the liberal approach to the world. "Hundreds of police, in full riot gear, police snipers on tops of buildings. Helicopters—Vietnam? NO! The entire South campus has been closed so that Roger Heyns can build a soccer field. The land belongs to the people who have created the beauty that is the park. By our love and sweat, we have built something of incalculable value for the entire community," reads a leaflet. (It really wasn't all that hard. No doubt there was sweat. There always is in Berkeley, where showers are not popular. And the climate in May is warm. But certainly no more sweat than any suburbanite works up when he digs his garden. And the thing itself, when finished, wasn't really exceptionally striking, no more striking than any rather shabby makeshift picnic ground. But in retrospect it took on all the qualities of Versailles. Said Alan Temko, who's called an "environmentalist" and according to his reputation is supposed to know about such things, "The People's Park is the most significant innovation in recreational design since the great public parks of the nineteenth and early twentieth century, such as Central Park in New York, Fairmont Park in Philadelphia, and Golden Gate Park in San Francisco." Now, this is completely whacky. Were you to put the People's Park into Central Park, the maintenance crew would sweep it up.)

"Students: meet Berkeley mothers and children at Sproul Plaza for the noon rally," the leaflet concludes. There's a lot of mileage in outraged mothers. "As moral people," says another leaflet, also aimed at the ladies, "you can't let them crush the youth this way. If you agree that things are not as they should be, that people without money or influence are powerless, that this must change in America, that the park was a constructive, creative act, an answer to our frustration and anger, then don't shop here today." (A citywide boycott of businesses had been urged to put pressure on the city council to intercede for the radicals.) "Those who brought the troops down on us on May 15 were horrified that the Community made use of a piece of land which belongs to everyone, without asking permission, just as the Southern slaveholders were horrified that their slaves took their liberty without permission." Surely such "logic" strains credulity, but this is just the sort of thing the liberals love. Those poor kids. Just like those poor slaves. And don't we just *loathe* southerners? And therefore Reagan? And so what if the land did not, in fact and in law, belong to everyone. Those poor kids. "There are jeeps mounted with machine guns and detention camps waiting for us. The big boys want to trap us in the streets so that they can get rid of us now—so that we will never have the chance to grow in numbers and take over." Well, *that's* a bit embarrassing. We don't actually want them to *take over,* do we? But that's just hyperbole. What's logical are those detention camps.

And it worked again, especially when some of the big-gun liberal national marshmallow minds showed up to second the militants. Linus Pauling, science's own Dr. Spock, leading a march of thousands of demonstrators to Sacramento, spoke from the capitol steps: "The evil war in Vietnam, the ABM, continued exploitation of the poor by the rich . . . the military-industrial complex is responsible for the evil episode that took place at Berkeley." That little makeshift picnic plot has become Vietnam.

Thus spoke a widely respected figure who has had much to do with the shaping of student minds. And his message was exactly that message delivered by the New Left revolutionaries. "I would like to be able to get into a dialogue on these grievances," Reagan had said to the demonstrators. "We are not interested in a dialogue with a murderer," responded Jim Hawley, a student who, along with Pauling, led the demonstrators. And on the same day demonstrators kicked, beat, and ripped up a stuffed effigy of Ronald Reagan. "Fuck Ronald Reagan," they screamed as they capered wildly around the effigy, snarling and tearing. And suppose that tool of the military-industrial complex, Ronald Reagan, were later on in the day to be assassinated by some crazed demonstrating lumpen. Would Dr. Pauling take credit for helping to create the atmosphere in which assassination would be possible? Of course not. Only right-wingers create such atmospheres.

This was all for liberal consumption. Among themselves, however, the New Leftists were a little more direct. One leaflet, issued by a coalition of the leftist groups, read in part: "Last Thursday we were given a very practical demonstration of the truth that 'all political power grows out of the barrel of a gun'. . . . We must fight back. We must refuse to be intimidated. We must be disciplined, and in an organized mass way resist the ban of rallies and meetings, the curfew and other fascist measures . . . if you don't have a gun, get one and learn to use it. . . . A .357 magnum or a .38 special revolver, a .45 caliber or 9mm automatic are good handguns; the M-1 or AR-15 rifles or M-1 carbine are good for longer ranges, and a 12 gauge shotgun with 00 buckshot—the same the pigs use—is good for self-defense at close range." The pamphlet ends with an instruction to "reach informed groups to discuss and apply the thoughts of Mao Tse-tung."

Even the most liberal reader must agree with this cautious statement made in the Reagan report: "It must be acknowledged that there are militants active within this state and this nation whose avowed aim is to destroy the institutions and the governmental structure of our society. They make no secret of these goals." Certainly not an extreme statement. Consider, for instance, the thirteen-point program drawn up by the New Left coalition shortly after People's Park:

1) **WE WILL MAKE TELEGRAPH AVENUE AND THE SOUTH CAMPUS A STRATEGIC FREE TERRITORY FOR THE REVOLUTION**
   . . . We will resist plans to destroy the South Campus through University-business expansion and pig assaults. . . . Young people leaving their parents will be welcome with full status as members of our community. Business on the Avenue should serve the humanist revolution by contributing their profits to the community. We will establish cooperative stores of our own, and combine them within an Avenue cooperative.

2) **WE WILL CREATE OUR REVOLUTIONARY CULTURE EVERYWHERE**
   . . . We will defy all puritanical restraints on culture and sex. . . .

3) **WE WILL TURN THE SCHOOLS INTO TRAINING GROUNDS FOR LIBERATION**

166

THE KUMQUAT STATEMENT

... Students must destroy the senile dictatorship of adult teachers and bureaucrats. Grading, tests, tracking, demotions, detentions and expulsions must be abolished. Pigs and narcs have no place in a people's school. . . . Students will establish independent educational forums to create revolutionary consciousness while continuing to struggle for change in the schools.

4) WE WILL DESTROY THE UNIVERSITY UNLESS IT SERVES THE PEOPLE

... Students should not recognize the false legal, in other words authority of the regents, administration, and faculty. All students have the right to learn what they want, from whom they want, and in the manner they decide; and the right to take political action without academic penalty. ... Education can only begin when we're willing to close the University for what we believe. . . .

5) WE WILL STRUGGLE FOR THE FULL LIBERATION OF WOMEN AS A NECESSARY PART OF THE REVOLUTIONARY PROCESS

... We demand the full control of our own bodies and towards that end will establish free birth control and abortion clinics. We will choose our own sexual partners. . . . We will establish female communes. . . .

6) WE WILL TAKE COMMUNAL RESPONSIBILITY FOR BASIC HUMAN NEEDS

... Free legal services will be expanded. Survival needs such as crash pads, free transportation, switchboards, free phones, and free food will be met.

7) WE WILL PROTECT AND EXPAND OUR DRUG CULTURE

... We relate to the liberating potential of drugs for both the mind and the body politic. Drugs inspire us to new possibilities in life which can be realized in revolutionary action. We intend to establish a drug distribution center and a marijuana cooperative. . . . We will resist the enforcement of all drug laws in our community. . . .

8) **WE WILL BREAK THE POWER OF THE LAND-LORDS AND PROVIDE BEAUTIFUL HOUSING FOR EVERYONE**

. . . Through rent strikes, direct seizures of property and other resistance campaigns, the large landlords, banks and developers who are gouging higher rents and spreading ugliness will be driven out. We shall force them to transfer housing control to the community. . . . Space will be opened up and living communes and revolutionary families will be encouraged.

9) **WE WILL TAX THE CORPORATIONS, NOT THE WORKING PEOPLE**

. . . Berkeley cannot be changed without confronting the industries, banks, insurance companies, railroads and shipping interests dominating the Bay Area. . . . We will demand a direct contribution from business, including Berkeley's biggest business—the University—to the community until a nationwide assault on big business is successful. . . .

10) **WE WILL DEFEND OURSELVES AGAINST LAW AND ORDER**

. . . We shall abolish the tyrannical police forces not chosen by the people. States of emergency, martial law, conspiracy charges and all the legalistic measures used to crush our movement will be resisted by any means necessary—from courtroom to armed struggle. The people of Berkeley must arm themselves and learn the basic skills and tactics of self defense and street fighting. . . . We shall make Berkeley a sanctuary for rebels, outcasts and revolutionary fugitives. . . .

11) **WE WILL CREATE A SOULFUL SOCIALISM IN BERKELEY**

. . . We will experiment with the new ways of living together such as communal families in which problems of income, child care and housekeeping are mutually shared. . . .

12) WE WILL CREATE A PEOPLE'S GOVERNMENT
. . . We will not recognize the authority of the bureaucratic and unrepresentative local government. We will ignore elections involving trivial issues and personalities. . . . We propose a referendum to dissolve the present government, replacing it with a decentralized government of neighborhood councils, workers councils, student unions, and different sub-cultures. . . .

13) WE WILL UNITE WITH OTHER MOVEMENTS THROUGHOUT THE WORLD TO DESTROY THIS MOTHERFUCKING RACISTCAPITALIST-IMPERIALIST SYSTEM
. . . We will make the American revolution with the mass participation of all the oppressed and exploited people. We will actively support the 10-point program of the Black Panther Party in the black colony. . . . We will create an international Liberation School in Berkeley as a training center for revolutionaries. . . .

Certainly a program for revolution. To easterners and midwesterners it sounds exaggerated. These are, after all, just hairy, funny-looking, middle-class brats. It's business as usual for those people who live and work in Manhattan or Des Moines, and the Berkeley New Left is really too exotic to be taken seriously. But if you visit Berkeley, or for that matter anywhere in the whole Bay Area, you take them a bit more seriously. Indeed, they've already partially realized most of their thirteen points.

Telegraph Avenue and the South Campus are now virtually a free revolutionary territory; the schools, even the junior highs, have become radicalized; the university has not been destroyed, but it is mortally wounded; drugs are as common as chocolate milk shakes used to be; the New Leftists and street people are successfully defending themselves against law and order—police these days fear to make arrests in the South Campus area; the Berkeley campus certainly is, if nothing else, an International Liberation School, a sanctuary and training base for rebels, outcasts, and revolutionary fugitives.

The radicals have very nearly captured one university and its community. And if they succeed at Berkeley they'll be looking for new territory. Wherever there are universities and kids they have potential bases. And if the People's Park proves anything, it proves how quickly and thoroughly the new culture can put down roots.

9

The new sensibility has become a political factor.

—Herbert Marcuse, *Essay on Liberation*

Dig it, first they killed those pigs [Sharon Tate and her group] and then they ate dinner in the same room with them, then they even shoved a fork into the victim's stomach. Wild!

—Bernadine Dohrn, SDS leader

Paul Glusman, writing in the underground newspaper *Rat,* encapsulates in a striking analogy what seems to me to be the present national state of mind. "Leon Trotsky," writes Glusman, "in his book on the Russian Revolution, describes the Petrograd bourgeoisie going to the opera and ballet the night after the fall of the Winter Palace unwilling to realize that they too would be caught in the events happening around them."

There are times, brought on by some obscure item buried back in the *New York Times* or by some brief news note on the transistor—a riot, a couple of buildings blown up—when reality gets close. But the explosions are comfortably muffled when you slip rapidly from house to train to office and back again. Add good food and several good strong martinis and a nightcap or two, and you really hear nothing at all. So it is too often with me. And so it is with all those newspaper, magazine, radio, and television men who control the national media from their eastern cocoons. Some of them hear the explosions, of course, but they come through the cocoon walls in a low, distant sort of way.

Hard, indeed, to hear anything through the walls of a cocoon. But it's out there. Listen to that rock music, which provides the kids with their phraseology, their philosophy, their life-style, the ideas and attitudes that motivate them and with which they explain the world. The dudes, jet-setters, and swingers hear the same music, take up the groups, twist and writhe to the sounds in those little joints they hang out in. But *they* don't hear the words. The kids do. Listen carefully, for instance, to Jefferson Airplane, so popular among the kids and the dudes alike:

> We are all outlaws in the eyes of Amerika
> In order to survive, we steal, cheat, lie, forge, fuck,
> hide and deal
> We are obscene, lawless, hideous, dangerous, dirty,
> violent and young.

They sing it so sweetly. And the dudes love it, squirming in their discotheques and at their parties, each one eventually ending up in bed with some other tired dude with early-morning halitosis. But for the dudes it's all sensation. For the kids, it's sensation as philosophy, sensation directed against something despicable.

Listen to what the kids hear. We hear the beat, the pulsing vitality in some cases, the sweetness in others. But the kids hear sounds and lyrics, and they're putting them together. Listen to the typical account of a Rolling Stones concert at Madison Square Garden, printed in a recent *Berkeley Barb*: "His Securityhood and Peeg drags from the stage a girl reaching the violent climax of masturbation while a thousand others who charged the stage and didn't make it mash one another in the pit—a freaked-out amoeba of human flesh downing joints and chewing minced poppy seeds. Convulsions, spasms, fists. . . 'I can't get nooo—SA—TIS—FAC—TION!' . . . The only satisfaction that's left in the old culture is watching it writhe and collapse, watching Mick Jagger impersonate its writhing and collapse, hearing Jagger's moan which is a death moan and not the moan of orgasm. . . . 'Satisfaction' feels good because it says how really bad things are. There's no satisfaction in school, in bed, in the Army, on the job, in the movies. . . . The whole audience is moving heavy because the song is something they can feel. Total revulsion at the death and sterility of bourgeois life and the demand for some way out.

"The lights go on. Everyone is up out of his seat, hands clapping; people are dancing. Everything is ready to bust loose. And then comes the Stones' last song. It's always 'Street Fighting Man'—in San Diego, in Denver, in Chicago, in New York. In Chicago Mick introduced 'Street Fighting Man' with the words, 'This is for you and what you did for your city.' In New York, a huge Amerikan flag hangs over the audience. And then there's that line, he sings it more than once, 'The time is ripe for violent revolution.' So our fists fly and Mick grins at the salute. And Mick snarls something bad.

"It's a turn-on badness. Don't matter how nice we were at Woodstock or Washington. Everyone of us knows somewhere inside that the time will come when we'll have to be very bad indeed. Eldridge Cleaver: 'Huey Newton is the baddest motherfucker ever to step inside the pages of history.' White history is just a few years behind. Our badness is coming. People gotta have satisfaction. People don't wait too long. People pick up guns. People smash states. People make the Revolution."

That's what they're hearing and feeling, all those twelve-, thirteen-, fourteen-, fifteen-year-olds who borrow daddy's car and a few bucks and drive off to a "concert." It's more than just music. It's philosophy, literature, and a program for action, all wrapped up in one emotional package. Visit Berkeley and look at the kids, the young ones. Junior high school girls with eyes as knowing and dead as any prostitute's. They've had it all, they know things at thirteen that we didn't learn until our twenties. They've experienced it all, years before they were mentally ready, and by the late teens they're jaded. They never will get any satisfaction, for they've experienced it before they should, and when they reach the age at which they're mentally ready it's behind them. So they'll rebel. No normal satisfaction for them, but the ideologists are there ready to show them how to get some new kicks. Revolution can be a legitimate response to unbearable conditions; it can also be an externalization of individual internal frustration. So we'd better listen very carefully to that music the kids are hearing. They're already socially and emotionally radicalized. The next step is politicization.

"WE WILL CREATE OUR REVOLUTIONARY CULTURE EVERYWHERE," one of the thirteen points goes. It is happening right under our noses. Once confined pretty much to Berkeley and the Bay Area, the culture has spread throughout the state of California and farther. Down in Reagan country, actress Sharon Tate, her unborn child, and four people in her home were butchered, then tied together, and on the walls of her home the word "PIG" was scrawled in blood. Word is that these people got their kicks by flirting with the more bizarre practices of the new culture. But the new culture finally got them. A weirdie named Charles Manson has been accused of masterminding the murders. Manson is the leader of an itinerant hippie cult that lived a nomadic life, sometimes in the Haight-Ashbury–Telegraph-Avenue milieu, sometimes out in the desert. He claimed at times to be God and at times Satan. A British cult that venerates God, Satan, and animals, the Process, claims that Manson was involved with them. The Process, an offshoot of the London-based Church of Scientology, an organization big on Telegraph, recently made a tour of the United States and claims to have made two hundred California converts.

The Processeans are vegetarians, pot smokers, and dress in black costumes with red devils on the collars. They wear thick silver crosses and swastika rings and hold special masses at which they worship Satan. All perfectly routine in the new culture. There is a Satanic church in Berkeley and the Satanists often speak on campus. No one finds it in the least odd. In the new culture Charles Manson is the model citizen. According to police reports, Manson and his group, whom the police connect with numerous other murders, believed that by murdering Sharon Tate they were liberating their victims from the condition of affluence in which they wallowed. When the police moved in on the cult, the girls were naked or bikini clad and wore knives in sheaths. There were also two babies suffering from malnutrition.

Not long ago, a lost wandering girl took refuge in the Haight-Ashbury and was befriended by several dope pushers. One night there was a party, and the girl was attacked by a half-dozen people who performed unnatural sex acts on her, ripping her insides and eventually killing her. According to some accounts, the sex acts continued after she died. Read the West Coast papers carefully. Such incidents are common.

The Mansons and the Satanists and the rapists are not New Leftists, of course, but their society is one that provides the New Left with its brown shirts. They can't get any satisfaction, and they've decided that the fault lies with society. So they've vowed to rip it up. The New Leftists are ideologists; the Mansons are not. But they accept common social forms and mores. They both advocate a drug culture, the Mansons and the Timothy Learys for what they believe is a resulting expansion of mystical consciousness, the New Leftists for those "new possibilities in life which can only be realized in revolutionary action." Both believe in communal living: Leary, perhaps, because it's the only way he can get his share of young chicks, Manson for reasons that perhaps only a psychologist can explain but which he no doubt thinks of as mystical, the New Leftists because communal living is a Marxist practice designed to break down the bourgeois notion of the family and private property. They look alike, sound alike, and are joined in their hatred of the system. Whatever the reasons, neither group can get satisfaction in the old culture. They are united in their hatred of it and their determination to bring it down. The New Leftists represent the political consciousness of the new culture, the Mansons and the Learys the religious. From a strictly Marxist point of view, an unlikely alliance. But leftist revolutionaries are never timid about forming any alliance that serves their ends. And in a neoromantic period, the political often unites with the mystical. There was probably no greater practitioner of realpolitik in this century than Hitler. But Hitler also had his Alfred Rosenberg and his astrologers.

And remember that Manson has recorded a rock album in prison. It will be a best seller and kids across the country will listen to it. A new folk hero in the country of the kids. And no doubt those squares and dudes will be humming along and dancing their intercourse-substitute, belly-rubbing dances to it. Sharon Tate would have loved it.

And listen to those bombs going off, though the sound is muffled inside those cocoons. We read in *Time* and in other periodicals that the massacres in Vietnam are all tied up with the shortcomings of our national character and the evil that inheres in our social system. But buildings have been blowing up in New York, and not even David Brinkley and Walter Cronkite seem to make the same sort of connection. It should be clear to anyone who has ever visited Berkeley or has even looked very carefully about him in New York that there is something very obvious linking up such things as the demolition of Berkeley's Wheeler Hall, the physical violence of the New Left movement, the casual slaughter of Sharon Tate, and the New York explosions. For all these actions have one thing in common: they are all social and political expressions of the new culture. Jane Alpert, for instance, the New York girl charged as one of the principals in the Manhattan bombings, attended Swarthmore and Columbia, and by her own admission was radicalized during the SDS uprising of 1968. She became a writer for the underground paper *Rat* and an active member of the New Left. She moved into an East Village pad with her boyfriend, and she has been prominent at various New York demonstrations held under flying Vietcong flags. A typical product of the new culture. And as soon as she got out on bail there was a Village rock festival held in her honor. And all the dudes and squares were there. "She's so *interesting!*"

179

There are other sounds. Sometimes, if you're in New York and you're bored and sober and have your wits about you, turn on your radio when the sun is a few hours below the horizon and move the dial around. A couple of New York stations that pretend to be total news stations run a half-dozen brief items over and over again. Others are supercilious talk shows, commercials, a few kids' stations with deejays shrieking and playing loud screaming obscenities, a classical music station featuring a fruity announcer with a travel agent voice.

But in between those New York frequencies, there are hundreds of other stations. Wheeling, Nashville, Louisville, and points south, Pittsburgh, Cincinnati, Des Moines, and, on a good clear night, Del Rio, Texas. The songs about truck drivers and waitresses and husbands who blow their whole check on a gin mill waitress while some sweet little thing waits weeping at home. And the tears in the beer—Iron City beer, Bulldog beer, Grain Belt beer, Coors. Generations of American fighting men, listening in tents to those tunes over Armed Forces Radio Service. There's a hell of a lot of them. And they're tough when they're roused, suddenly wild, stomping, gouging, shooting tough, tough in a way that so far only overseas enemies have seen.

Increasingly, these men are coming to view the domestic enemy as the equivalent of the foreign. The cocoon dwellers don't seem to notice that when they and their neighbors march in one of those nice antiwar parades organized by those nice radicals like David Dellinger that they invariably march under Vietcong banners carried by those nice boys from the campuses. But those cowboys out there see them, and in their eyes the banner carriers are despicable punks, pampered brats of well-to-do families, not a muscle built by work in their bodies, a spoiled bunch whose daddies' money has bought extended adolescence and long leisure work-less times to roam around tearing down the campuses that offer them privileged sanctuary.

There are the enlisted men out there, the fighters who have kept American society whole by surrendering certain liberties and following the directives of elected authority. In wartime they obey their officers and in peacetime they obey their officials, for this is the only way that democracy can function. But democracy is fragile, as the New Leftists who challenge it know. And when and if it comes through to the enlisted men that their officers have lost authority, if these officers by bow-ing to the wishes of a revolutionary minority lose the moral basis of their authority, then the enlisted men will take matters into their own hands. Once the troops have mutinied, it will be very difficult indeed to bring them back into line. And while theirs is a tradition of obedi-ence to just authority for the good of America, there is an equally strong tradition of vigilanteeism. The gun-fighter is as important an American figure as GI Joe.

The American enlisted man, the American working-man, prizes those values—honesty, patriotism, thrift, dignity in work—that we call typically American more highly than any of his officers do. His life has been shaped by our culture, he is its greatest champion, and he em-braces completely its values and the standards that grow out of these values. To such people, the New Leftists are the exact antithesis of everything worth prizing. They understand what the New Leftists admit, loudly and clearly, day after day, at every rally and in every one of their numerous publications—they want to bring America down, they want it to be humiliated, they want that machine to be smashed. They want the Vietcong to win, not because they have anything at all in common with them (imagine a VC meeting a Berkeley New Leftist— he'd pen him up and put him on exhibit in the Hanoi Zoo) but because they want us to get beaten.

The cocoon dwellers don't understand this at all. They are officers, like the officers of Czarist Russia in 1917 or France in 1936, who have lost touch with their troops. The troops know, however. Those aren't reformers out there. Those are revolutionaries who want to rip everything up. And to hell with what replaces it. Appease them and they'll be back the next day with even more outrageous demands. And this had better penetrate those cocoons soon. Otherwise the troops are going to get tired of waiting for their officers and do the job themselves. And they may just decide to rip up those cocoons, too.

The Liberty Lobbyists and the National Youth Alliance, both groups that make the John Birchers look like liberals, grow stronger daily. It's building, and unless the trend is reversed it's all going to blow.

What can we do? Some steps are obvious. The war on society is still being waged from bases on university campuses. University administrators could address themselves to cleaning up their institutions. They needn't be repressive. Few universities in the country do not have existing regulations that, if enforced, could effectively curb the radicals. Hayakawa did it. And university governing boards have the legal right to weed out openly subversive professors.

In society at large, there are more than enough laws—antinarcotics, antivagrancy, antiarson, antiriot, and so on—to handle destroyers. All that is necessary is the will to enforce these laws. Most of the people on Telegraph Avenue daily violate dozens of existing laws in the full view of the police. But the police need support.

No doubt the liberals would call stiff enforcement of existing laws "repression." But when their kids become addicts and enough of their commuting trains blow up, perhaps they could just call those New Leftists right-wingers and righteously demand law and order.

10

Violence alone, violence committed by the people, violence organized and educated by its leaders, makes it possible for the masses to understand social truths and gives the key to them.

—Frantz Fanon, *The Wretched of the Earth*

Let's understand what's going on. We're engaged in a guerrilla war and a revolutionary situation is building fast. One spark, I fear, falling on the right ground at the right time, could kick it off in earnest.

And if it happens, it will be extremely violent. Our toleration for violence increases rapidly. Daniel Bell, a liberal academic who, like all liberal academics, has long had his guns trained in the wrong direction, wrote in the 1950s: "Barbarous acts are rarely committed out of the blue. (As Freud says, first one commits oneself in words, then in deeds.) Step by step, a society becomes accustomed to accept, with less and less moral outrage and with greater and greater indifference to legitimacy, the successive blows."

Bell wrote, of course, of the violence he felt was coming from the right. But the psychological analysis is sound and the process he describes is the process that has gradually clouded liberal wits at Berkeley. It is the same process that allows the cocoon dweller to remain relatively unruffled as the world blows up around him. (I have no doubt whatsoever that by the time this book is published we'll all have grown accustomed to urban

187

terror bombings.) And it's the same process that has caused the liberal establishment to sanction violence.

Early in 1970, an important article appeared in *Harper's* magazine. Entitled "The Future of American Violence," it was written by Columbia's Richard Hofstadter, perhaps the single most important remaining spokesman for the academic liberal orthodoxy. Hofstadter, like Theodore White a year earlier, has finally had to admit that not only is there violence in America, but that the violence comes from the left.

It's a terribly hard admission for Professor Hofstadter to make, for it contradicts the views upon which he built his reputation. Through the fifties and into the sixties, Hofstadter and his colleagues have been waiting for the right to explode. That it would was monolithically believed in academe, and the Hofstadters spent nearly two decades preparing us for rightist violence in scores of books and articles. But, as it turned out, their warnings were as meaningless as those of Colonel Robert R. McCormick, who used to warn us of impending invasion from Canada.

The right-wingers, Daniel Bell believed, were just waiting for the right moment "to tear apart the fabric of society." Hofstadter agreed wholeheartedly and invariably described members of the right as "the radical right," "self-styled conservatives," "pseudo-conservatives," "ultra-conservatives." (It's interesting that there is no corresponding terminology for labeling leftists. Ever hear anyone described as an "ultra-liberal" or a "pseudo-liberal" or a "self-styled liberal"? There is the "radical left," of course, but there is also the "responsible left," while the conservatives are never allowed responsible members. And, of course, the word "liberal" is not constantly qualified with a pejorative adjective.) In article after

188

article we were prepared. There was Joe McCarthy, all set to tear things apart. There was Robert Welch. There were the Minutemen.

A few years ago this strange single-sighted ability to see only out of the left eye bothered me terribly, and I was certain that it was intentional, that by discrediting the right the leftists hoped to impose their rigid ideological vision of the good gray, completely conformist, semi-Marxian welfare state on everyone. But I no longer believe this. I rather think that the problem is mainly a combination of social simplemindedness and acute liberal schizophrenia. The latter, in particular, seems the best way to characterize the strange state of mind that shapes Professor Hofstadter's essay on violence. And the use of a psychological term seems particularly apt in discussing Hofstadter, for he himself enjoys using them when discussing the right.

Professor Hofstadter has long worried about rightist mental health. A few years ago he decided that we were all paranoiacs. His diagnosis was made on the basis of style: "A distorted style is, then," he told us in *The Paranoid Style in American Politics,* "a possible signal that may alert us to a distorted judgment, just as an ugly style is a cue to fundamental defects of taste. What interests me here is the possibility of using political rhetoric to get at political pathology."

Fine idea. Hofstadter gives us a few examples and ends up with a Joe McCarthy speech that does sound a bit unhinged, although not really terribly so when compared with the pathological political rhetoric of the sixties. Take this, for instance, spoken by Eldridge Cleaver from exile: "The fascists have already declared the murder of Chairman Bobby Seale [who has been receiving kid-glove treatment in a New Haven court-

189

room] and all of the other members of our party. Our brothers are being murdered in their sleep. Our offices are subject to military attack. The fascist Nixon administration has unleashed the F.B.I. on us. Hundreds of party members are being picked up on false political charges. It is nothing but an attempt to sabotage the 400-year struggle for liberation. We black people must unleash the ultimate political consequences of this nation—race war."

The paranoid, Hofstadter told us, "believes himself to be living in a world in which he is spied upon, plotted against, betrayed, and very likely destined for total ruin."

When in 1970 Professor Hofstadter takes up his pen to write an essay on violence and the left, one expects him to bring the same acute psychological perceptions to his task that he had exercised a decade before. But he doesn't. Political pathology can indeed be sniffed out by analyzing rhetoric. But apparently only the rhetoric of the right.

Listen, for instance, to how gingerly Hofstadter treats H. Rap Brown. Says Professor Hofstadter: " 'Violence,' said Rap Brown in what must surely remain one of the memorable utterances of our time, 'is necessary and it's as American as cherry pie.' " One of the memorable utterances of our time.

Imagine Professor Hofstadter's reaction if Robert Welch were to say, "Violence is necessary and it's as American as peach pie" (we'll vary the clichés to keep the utterances "memorable" for Mr. Hofstadter); or if Barry Goldwater were to say, "Violence is necessary and it's as American as huckleberry pie"; or Richard Nixon, "Violence is necessary and it's as American as rhubarb pie." Imagine the horror, the outrage, the accusations of conservative paranoia. The ravings of extremists, Hofstadter would tell us.

The schizophrenia of the liberal left is acute, and Professor Hofstadter's article illustrates the seriousness of the illness. He begins by restating his favorite thesis, that there are and always have been "violence cults on the Right." The example he trots out, of course, is "European fascism" (which responsible conservatives have always eschewed; never forget the "socialism" in Hitler's "National Socialism"). He then quickly equates the whole American right with the fascists. The time-honored liberal smear. Isn't there something paranoid about the way the Hofstadters fear us?

Then, having dispatched the right in a fast paragraph, on to the left. What most surprises Hofstadter is "the decline of the commitment to nonviolence on the Left, and the growth of the disposition to indulge or to exalt acts of force or violence." But wait. The right is traditionally violent, the left traditionally nonviolent? It's a thesis that Hofstadter has consistently advanced throughout his academic career. But is it really true? Is there *really* a nonviolent leftist tradition? If he chooses to make Martin Luther King and Gandhi leftists, that gives him two. But no more. Was the Russian Revolution nonviolent? The Chinese? The Cuban? And has Hofstadter heard of Hungary? Czechoslovakia? How about the whole of Eastern Europe? Remember that fellow called Stalin? Ever hear of Tibet? Apparently not, for he repeats: "Historically, violence has not been an effective weapon of the Left. . . ." An odd statement for a historian, for it seems possible to argue just as effectively that violence has been the *only* effective weapon of the left; there are very few nations indeed in

191

which the majority of citizens have voluntarily chosen communism.

Having established by fiat his premises, he then proceeds to deliver what apparently constitutes the new liberal rationale for violence. And here his essay becomes most important—and most frightening: Violence is the everyday tool of the police and the military. "Under normal circumstances, violence has more characteristically served domineering capitalists or trigger-happy police, peremptory sergeants or fascist hoodlums." Notice that cute academic use of unqualified modifiers. Capitalists as a class are "domineering"; policemen as a class are "trigger-happy."

The "fascist hoodlums" (policemen and capitalists) are the real purveyors of violence. Violence comes "from the top of society." "The model for violence . . . has been the hideous and gratuitous official violence in Vietnam" (also, rightists "indulge" in violence, leftists "resort" to it). The Vietnam argument is standard but hardly logical. The kids use Vietnam as a model for violence? But we thought they were *opposed* to violence in Vietnam. According to Hofstadter's reasoning, New Leftists are resorting to violence in order to show their hatred of violence. That's rather like resorting to drunkenness to show your support of prohibition. What do views such as Hofstadter's lead to? Listen to a statement put out by New Leftists shortly after the William Kunstler-inspired Santa Barbara riots during which the quarter-million-dollar Bank of America building was burned to the ground:

> **We are deeply disturbed by the wanton acts of aggression perpetrated on the peoples of S. E. Asia engaged in revolutionary struggles. These military interventions are not childish pranks, peaceful demonstrations, nor even**

non-violent disruptions designed to give symbolic meaning to imperialism. Rather, they are criminal acts of violent proportions directed against the people's democratic struggle. They are fascist gestures of the kind that lead to further violence, bloodshed, and repression. Nor are they isolated instances but rather a continuation of the calculated violence that has been emanating from your banks and financial institutions in the name of the state under the directions of the corporate few. . . .

We accuse your bank, Chairman Lundborg and ex-chairman Peterson, in your plunder of "hungry new markets" and your affiliations with defense contractors like Litton and McDonnell-Douglas, in your magnanimous aid to the CIA through the Asia Foundation, of raping the "underdeveloped world". . . .

Your retail food outlets distribute food of declining quality, artificially grown, and of little nutritional value. We accuse you of destroying the world's ecological balance through your mining concerns, your manufacturing interests, and your petroleum companies like Union Oil (or have you forgotten the beaches of Santa Barbara?)

In whose interests is LAW and ORDER when one of your directors, Harry S. Baker, sits on the board of the largest police weapons manufacturer in the world. . . .

This is for the people of the world to decide: what is the burning of a bank compared to the founding of a bank? In whose interest is law and order when tyranny prevails?

ALL POWER TO THE PEOPLE

A lengthy statement, and drearily familiar to those accustomed to New Left rhetoric. But note the points it makes, the issues it raises. The directors of the Bank of America are Hofstadter's "domineering capitalists," "fascist hoodlums" who oppress the wretched of the world. Their violence is the only real violence; burning down buildings or blowing them up is not violent at all compared to the "violence" involved in founding the bank. (Or for that matter, the violence of selling food. Note the reference to "food of declining quality." Apparently you're justified in burning down the bank because stores sell sliced white bread.) Much less subtle than Hofstadter, of course, but *exactly* the same point. Capitalism is synonymous with violence. And thus the sophistical Marcusian redefinition of violence—what your side does is *never* really violent. And thus the intellectual surrender of the old liberal establishment to the radical New Left, a surrender that may well mark one of most significant turning points in American history. For here is one of the most respected and eloquent members of the liberal academic establishment tacitly excusing in advance any excesses committed by the New Leftists in places like Santa Barbara. The "fascist hoodlums" after all deserve it (you should never feel guilty about stomping a policeman to death, William Kunstler has said).

I suspect Professor Hofstadter thinks he's doing something completely different from what he in fact accomplishes. Having established to his satisfaction that he's all for the kids and doesn't give a hoot in hell what they detonate, he says: "No doubt it is tempting to think of putting a final end to some grave and massive social evil by a quick, surgical, limited act of violence." However, he continues, the problem is that radicals fail to show "a careful concern about when and how violence can be justified, or upon sober estimates of its past role or its prospects of future success." And suddenly you suspect he's actually trying to *lecture* them, trying to turn it all into a *subject,* something you can be "careful" and "sober" about.

No doubt he thinks he's going to help them simmer down. "Violence," he allows, "is not only useful but therapeutic [and how *good* they must have felt after burning down that bank or murdering that San Francisco policeman with a bomb]. But the restorative power of

194

violence . . . must surely depend upon its being used successfully. . . ." And it becomes pitifully clear what he thinks he's going to accomplish. He's going to grant that all the reasons the radicals advance for being violent are valid. He's with them. But he's going to argue also that they probably can't succeed. And why not? Because that bogeyman of the "radical right" who has been hiding under his bed for two decades is still there, itching to tear things up. The kids will just give them an excuse. The kids may be violent—they blow things up, shoot people, fire-bomb homes—but "the most serious danger comes not from the activities of young militants, black or white, but from the strength of the backlash that may arise out of an increasing polarization."

Now this is an interesting statement. If the last few weasel words mean what I might take them to mean, if Hofstadter is trying to say that people are finally going to get so sick of being terrorized in their communities by New Left guerrillas that they're going to fight back, then I agree. But I'm afraid that's not it at all. Rather, I fear, it's just another example of that famous inability to see the enemy on the left while imagining, in the most paranoid fashion, an ever mobilized enemy on the right, ready to march.

Of course, it is possible that Hofstadter really detests violence, but knowing he can't take the moral line is actually trying to reason them out of violence by arguing against violence only through expediency. And if he is, he deserves our profound pity, for this is precisely what every liberal academic who believes these kids love him has tried to do. I think of a recent example. The ROTC building at Washington University was burned to the ground by campus radicals. Asked to com-

195

ment, Chancellor Thomas Eliot said, "While I disapprove of violence, you've got to understand the way the kids feel about that bloody war in Vietnam." Two weeks later they burned down another building, sacked the administration building, destroyed irreplaceable files, and promised to burn the library down. At last report they had trapped Chancellor Eliot in his home, chanting "Ho, Ho, Ho Chi Minh, the NLF is gonna win" and "Let's hang Eliot." This is what inevitably happens to those liberal academics who try to make friends with the kids. They continue to believe that they can reason with them right up to that day when their offices go up in smoke.

Daniel Bell, collaborating with Hofstadter and others in *The Radical Right* (1962), tells us that "the crucial turning point comes when . . . social movements can successfully establish 'private armies' whose resort to violence—street fightings, bombings . . . cannot be controlled by the elected authorities, and whose use of violence is justified or made legitimate by the respectable elements in society." An excellent description, although misdirected at the menace on the right, of present conditions in America. Such groups—the Panthers, the SDS Weathermen, various "liberation" organizations—proliferate and behave in exactly the way foreseen by Mr. Bell. Listen, for instance, to the manifesto of the Black Liberation Front, an armed organization that recently took credit for ambushing three policemen who had committed the crime of being born white:

> **The Black Liberation Front is an organization of young men and women who are totally committed to Black people's liberation and self-actualization. Many of us experienced the frustration of the Civil Rights struggle that dominated the Sixties, and are determined to make the**

196

THE KUMQUAT STATEMENT

Seventies a period of significant change. We intend to
make 1970 the turning point in Black people's four-hun-
dred-year struggle for liberation.

WE HEREBY DECLARE THAT A STATE OF WAR
NOW EXISTS BETWEEN BLACK AMERICA AND
THE WHITE OPPRESSIVE INSTITUTIONS AND
FORCES THAT SUPPRESS BLACK PEOPLE'S STRUG-
GLE FOR FREEDOM.
Listed below are the basic demands of the BLF.
These demands are non-negotiable with the exception of the
one dealing with reparations.

1. TOTAL WITHDRAWAL OF ALL POLICE
FORCES from the Black Community to be replaced by the
BLF Army.
As a result of countless incidents of brutality, and the
general disregard for the welfare of the community that
characterize police behavior, we believe that the police
are a disservice to the community. Therefore, they should
be thrown out of our streets and replaced by our own people. The most damning evidence showing that the police
are not functioning in our best interests is their infiltration
of Black organizations that are struggling for our liberation.

2. TOTAL CONTROL of all schools, hospitals, and
public services within the Black community.
This would include establishing cooperative ownership
of all housing and businesses within the communities.

3. REPARATIONS amounting to the sum of three
billion, 900 million dollars. These reparations are essential for the development of an economically independent
Black community.

4. LIBERATION of all Black political prisoners.

5. EXTRATERRITORIAL RIGHTS for all Black
people arrested outside of their communities.
This means that if a Black man from Harlem is arrested in Forest Hills, his case must be tried in Harlem
with a jury composed of his peers.

Such outfits are forming all over the country, essentially private armies that meet all of Bell's criteria.

197

And by approving, no matter how abstractly, of militant violence, Professor Hofstadter is justifying it. The crucial moment comes, said Bell, when such violence "is justified or made legitimate by the respectable elements in society." And there is certainly no more "respectable element" in our society than the liberal bourgeois professoriat, of which Professor Hofstadter is an outstanding member. And this brings us to the most dangerous aspect of Professor Hofstadter's essay: by justifying violence he makes it extremely difficult for Bell's "elected authorities" to control it in any way whatsoever and by so doing vastly increases the possibility of the "backlash" he professes to fear.

I will explain by way of a rather lengthy anecdote. I was in Berkeley just after the Chicago 7 verdict came in. The city was jittery, more so than I could ever remember, with an air of suppressed violence bubbling just beneath the surface. When the verdict was announced, the kids gathered in Provo Park for a sympathy rally. They burned effigies of Judge Julius Hoffman and, as one militant tells it, "Somebody hoisted a burning garbage can to the top of the flag pole. It captured the feelings of everybody about our Amerika [sic], what it meant, what it is, and what's in store for it in the future."

The mob screamed and chanted and then stampeded, fifteen hundred of them, spilling onto Shattuck Avenue, downtown Berkeley's major business street, heaving rocks, bricks, and bottles, beating people in their path, smashing windows with clubs. It lasted for two hours, covered twenty-two blocks. A Safeway market was looted (a memorable moment came when black Safeway clerks counterattacked and, although outnumbered one hundred to one, drove the looters off) and the windows of all Berkeley's large banks were smashed in.

Even more seriously damaged were the small businesses —bookstores, barbershops, a candy store, a violin shop, a one-man private press, even a small home for old people. Many of these businesses have been forced to close down—the proprietors are hardly charter members of the military-industrial complex.

"It's the best riot we've ever had," cooed one coed from the university's Center for Participant Education (the same outfit that gave us Professor Cleaver). But nonacademic Berkeleyites disagreed, and in tones they've never before used. Liberal doveish Mayor Wallace Johnson said, "We can no longer continue to tolerate dissidents who insist on destroying society." Said liberal City Manager William Hanley, "Our two hundred policemen can't provide security in the face of this kind of depraved, psychopathic behavior." "For the past six years," said businessman Earl Cunha, summing up the feelings of most Berkeleyites, "a dangerous and anarchistic revolutionary minority has been doing its thing in Berkeley—twenty-two days of curfew, twenty days of street fighting, over $2.75 million in extra police costs, not to mention the terror struck into the hearts of old and young alike."

Indeed a "preview of the riots of the seventies"— just as at Santa Barbara, pure violence, and violence directed not at universities but at university cities. But perhaps also a preview of the reactions of the seventies. For in Berkeley, after the mindless rampage and random bombings, citizens, for the first time in a decade, were not content to stop at rhetoric. Petitions were circulated asking more rigid enforcement of existing laws, which could, if properly implemented, effectively contain the radicals; more official support of Berkeley's fine but demoralized police force ("I'm not sure I believe it," said one patrolman. "But if they really mean it, if they're really behind us, we can take anything the baboons dish out. With pleasure"); more official control over openly subversive and revolutionary groups; more sensible legal approaches to bail and sentencing. The petitions, in short, asked nothing more than that officials carry out their functions. And the response was astonishing. Over fifteen thousand citizens signed the petitions within a two-week period. Had they been circulated for another week, the number would have doubled.

The signers were *not* right-wingers. They had no ideological or political axes to grind. They were simply ordinary citizens of the city of Berkeley, tired of seeing their town periodically torn up in the name of whatever issue happened to be on hand at the time, tired of walking their own streets in fear. Like so many others across the country, they are fed to the teeth with liberal abstractionists who have for so long managed to blame everyone but rioters for riots, and by so doing have encouraged bigger and better riots. Officials in Berkeley have been given their orders by the police who elect them; all they need is the will to carry them out. One hopes fervently that they will muster up that will. For in Berkeley, and perhaps in much of the rest of the country, we may be getting close to the last chance.

EPILOGUE

We're going to get your children.

—Abbie Hoffman and Jerry Rubin

The killings at Kent State were horrifying. The post-Cambodian reaction was blowing the country. The campuses were exploding.

In a letter mailed to the *New York Times,* the Weathermen wrote: "The hundreds and thousands of young people who demonstrated in the sixties against the war and for civil rights grew to hundreds of thousands in the past few weeks actively fighting Nixon's invasion of Cambodia and the attempted genocide against black people. The insanity of Amerikan 'justice' has added to its list of atrocities six blacks killed in Augusta, two in Jackson and four white Kent State students making thousands more into revolutionaries."

The fury of the campuses at the Cambodia invasion was unprecedented, and for a period the entire nation seemed like one huge People's Park. And like People's Park there was that startling flash of insight, that sudden realization that people across the country were much closer to the brink of radicalization than any of us quite realized.

Almost overnight many universities dropped all pretense of objectivity and became centers for partisan political lobbying and propagandizing.

Reactions among those consciously nonideological and conservative professors and students to the universities' openly partisan stand were varied. At Columbia, then so radicalized that sixty-six of the sixty-eight varsity football players supported an all-university strike, and where students had to get passes from radicals to use the libraries, there was a sense of defeat among members of Students for Columbia University, moderates and conservatives who had joined forces to battle and often defeat academic disruption over the past few years. "What the radicals have tried to accomplish for four years," said one student, "the faculty and administration have done in a day." Another SCU student, senior David Carpenter, wrote an impassioned letter to the Columbia administration:

To the Administration of Columbia University:

Gentlemen:

Four years and over 8,000 dollars ago I came to Columbia College expecting to be able to get a good liberal arts education and in general spend my college years in the peaceful pursuit of this goal. We all have our dreams. In four years at Columbia I have witnessed the destruction of a once honorable institution. I have seen a once great university become a third-rate political tool for a mob of Vietcong flag waving animals who trample the rights of anyone who dares to disagree with them. This mob rules while the spineless "leaders" of the university community cringe under their desks (when they can get into the buildings) and talk about whether they are relevant or not. I have seen a once honored Columbia degree become a worthless scrap of paper while the only real leader Columbia ever had, Dr. Truman, gets the axe because he might offend the sensitivity of the mob. I have seen many of the university's best faculty members pack their bags and leave in frustration or fear or maybe simply because they don't

204

relish the thought of having their files burned. I have seen the last three spring semesters disrupted with the disrupters getting only a slap on the wrist by the administrators who so want to understand them. Gentlemen, I've seen all this and I've done my best to fight it. In 1968 I stood with the majority coalition when the university refused to act. I went to court against the trustees when we thought that might stir them to head off future disruptions. Last spring I acted with others to attempt to open up the buildings when it appeared that the administration was vacillating. Just a few weeks ago I stood with others in front of Hamilton Hall while the mob threw bricks at it to prevent them from smashing their way in. During the last three years I have had my life repeatedly threatened because I chose to stand against the mob. And now I'm finished.

Gentlemen, I've had enough. I'm throwing in the towel. I have fought for Columbia for the last four years and now I believe that there is nothing worth fighting for. Let your little friends wave their Vietcong flags. I'm sure my friends who went to Vietnam and never returned would appreciate their youthful idealism. Sit around and debate the war in your cozy senate meetings while Columbia slides into the cesspool. I no longer care. I am leaving Columbia this week to return to my native land, the United States of America, and I only hope its people will take me back.

I will not attend commencement. That would delay my departure too long and I can't get out of here soon enough. You may mail my diploma to my home address. . . . You have said that I should seek out my teachers and attempt to barter for a passing grade for my courses. This I refuse to do. I will not chase them all over the East Coast because they can't get into their classrooms or offices in this great university, which I am told by the president is still open. I have been told that I should try to finish my papers, but the last time I tried to get into the library I met a barrage of obscenities and was threatened with a club. . . . The academic environment or rather the lack of it at Columbia at this time makes any attempt at scholastic endeavor ludicrous. . . . I ask that you pass me for the semester and mail me my diploma. I believe it's the least you can do. You have completely failed in your duty to keep Columbia open and maintain an orderly academic environment. Thanks to you gentlemen further study at

Columbia this year is an impossibility. I realize that my request for a blanket pass for this semester is an unusual one, yet thanks to you gentlemen these are unusual times. If you deny my request for a B.A. degree for any reason I am quite prepared to take Columbia to Federal Court and sue as an out-of-state student. This is not meant as a threat or a bluff, merely a statement of fact. I will not allow you to penalize me because of your inability to keep the university open, which is your legal duty.

Gentlemen, I am angry and bitter, not at the leftists, who do what is predictable, but with you gentlemen. You have failed me and every other student who came to Columbia not for a war or to turn the university into a political tool for his pet cause, but for an education. For those like me Columbia is no longer worth fighting for—not when those whose duty it is to protect her fail to meet any crisis with courage and leadership. Gentlemen, continue with your myth that Columbia is still open, even though you can't get into your offices and the students can't get into the library. I want no more of it. In closing I ask only the right to leave in peace, to go on to law school elsewhere and try to forget the fact that I was fool enough to fight for Columbia for four bitter years.

Dave Carpenter left at the end of May, after receiving a death threat and a pig's head in the morning mail.

Nevertheless, there are small but significant signs that a campus counterrevolution may be stirring. Many students are taking the lawsuit route. Students at Washington University are suing the university for $7,700,000 for failure to "prevent the repeated disruption of classes and other educational activities." At Stanford, the Free Campus Movement is suing for $1,050,000 in actual and punitive damages. The Stanford students were beaten by a mob of radicals during the recent uprisings. Lawsuits have also been instituted at Marymount College, George Washington law school, Wayne State, and Adelphi, to mention just a few. New groups of moderate but nonideological students are proliferating. At Hofstra and

Dartmouth they call themselves Strike Back. A group called Students for Responsible Action is petitioning the presidents of a number of colleges to act against illegal strikes. Similar petitions are being circulated at Mount Saint Mary College and at Harvard. And at Smith, students have addressed an open letter to the members of their community that cogently sums up the feelings of the majority of moderate students about the rash of campus lockouts. The letter reads:

> To the Smith College community: We who endorse this statement represent a wide spectrum of views concerning the many substantive issues raised by the Strike Committee. However, we are united by our objection to a strike within an academic community—
> Our reasons are as follows:
> 1) It is not the college's place as an institution of higher education to take a stand on political issues, thereby losing its freedom to view all sides of any issue in its search for truth.
> 2) The impelling emotionalism which has obscured the issues is equally repugnant to the ideals of academic objectivity.
> 3) The disruption of the objective educational process for a one-sided presentation of political issues is a denial of the equal academic opportunity that has been guaranteed to all students.
> 4) Everyone, from time to time, has felt strong political commitments. However, we object to the fact that, for the first time, academic regulations have been relaxed for those who hold such commitments. It is not necessary to suspend one type of education in order to provide for another.
> 5) We further object to the use of student government machinery to facilitate strike machinery.
> 6) The atmosphere engendered by the strike is not conducive to the pursuit of academic endeavors. Personal or group pressure inflicted upon those who wish to continue their work is repressive and an infringement of an individual's freedom, and not to be tolerated on or off the campus.

> Having made this statement, we are now going back
> to work and hope that others will have the freedom to do
> the same.

A striking statement, embodying many points I've tried to make in this book. All that conservatives who lament the current condition of academe really want, after all, is a community of scholars, in which a realistic concept of academic freedom is the guiding principle. This is impossible at today's multiversity. Recently I went to the University of Buffalo. With the possible exception of Cornell, no university east of the Mississippi has been so racked by turmoil. Buffalo is as Berkeley was half a decade ago. During the 1969–70 academic year there seemed to be a riot a week, complete with arson, fire-bombings, and, on at least one occasion, sniper fire. I visited Buffalo to find out what was happening and why. What I found was chaos. "Our students are full of distrust, our faculty in disarray and our administrative leaders inaccessible," reads a faculty report. "These conditions are making it extremely difficult to start talking with each other." True enough, although after my visit I came to realize that the problem isn't that people aren't talking; they're talking up a storm. The problem is similar to the problem that afflicts every multiversity campus in the country: No one is listening.

A few examples: It's late at night and we're sitting in the back room of a Buffalo beer joint, talking to the leader of Buffalo's SDS, a bunch of militants and easy riders, and a liberal faculty member. The talk is basic— revolution, the rationale for violence, bombs, how conservatives will be shot by New Leftists when the crunch comes, how liberal faculty will be put against the wall even sooner. The liberal faculty member touches my arm and smiles at everyone in general. "See," he tells me in a confidential tone, "we can communicate with the kids, can't we?"

Another conversation with SDS and friends, this time in the Student Union building, one of those modular, sealed-window, contemporary collegiate, controlled-air buildings in which there's never quite enough air to breathe.

"We don't really care who runs the university," says an SDSer. "Universities are our bases now."

"Universities should be vortices in which intelligent people may disagree with neither contumely nor violence, in an atmosphere of courtesy, mutual respect and collegiality," says the professor.

"Thank God for liberal professors," mutters one militant, grinning into his beer.

"My objection to disruption is essentially the same as my objection to racial prejudice," says the professor. "It's all just bad manners."

A lovely, fragile seventeen-year-old coed with china eyes sits down and tells the professor, "It's my country, but I hate it now. Just look at what they did to Professor Fiedler. I really learned from him." The coed leaves.

"See?" smiles the professor. "You can *talk* to these kids."

The SDSer sips his beer. "We'll have her in a week," he says. He gets up, shakes my hand, and tells me he's going to hate to shoot me, come the crunch.

The professor smiles.

Paranoia is rife at the multiversity. Administrators suspect both their colleagues and the faculty of conspiring against them. And every student, of course, is a potential bomb thrower. And everyone *knows* that wild-eyed right-wingers lurk about the campus, ready to attack. And faculty groups suspect that state governments are plotting to reduce their rather splendid salaries. Students believe faculty has sold them out, that administrators plot with the Defense Department and the military-industrial complex to oppress "the people."

In the meantime no one learns anything, for in such an atmosphere education is impossible.

The problems that afflict the multiversity are bigness, overcentralization, and purposelessness. The handwriting has been on the wall ever since Clark Kerr first described the multiversity as a large machine, the least function of which was to educate students. He was answered shortly thereafter by Mario Savio, who called upon students to stop the machine. Which they have begun to do.

But at the end of the fifties into the sixties, during the last great flowering of social scientism, no one was listening. In the sixties the California multiversity system became *the* pattern, and it is this pattern that New York State has emulated. The State University of New York (SUNY) system, according to the master plan, would consist of four university centers, two medical centers, ten colleges of arts and sciences, at least seven specialized colleges, thirty community colleges. All of this would be inhabited by a student population of 300,000 and the whole thing would be run by one man. The state legislature threw in the money like confetti. "Filthy rich," wrote Barbara Probst Solomon, in *Harper's* magazine, "it [SUNY] is buying up scholars and, along with them, super-salesmen who have no idea what they are selling or why. . . ."

Faculty stars—at Buffalo, men like Leslie Fiedler,

John Barth, Robert Creely—traded their talents for stunningly short workweeks—an average of six hours—and fat salaries. Even assistant professors at Buffalo clear better than $12,000 for a nine-month year. The fact is that high salaries and small work loads leave the majority of multiversity professors with time on their hands.

And then, of course, you find educational hucksters, failed administrators, men who talk the same old rhetoric they've been spouting since the thirties, the accepted educationist jargon, the verbal smoke screen that conceals the inability to cope with basic problems confronting higher education.

The big lesson to be learned from Berkeley and Buffalo and all similar campuses is, essentially, this: In times of stress, the multiversity simply isn't workable. At nearly every large university that has experienced similar prolonged disruption, presidents and chancellors pass the buck to trustees and regents, who in turn pass it on to governors and politicians. Lines of communication and control blur dramatically when crisis hits. And muddling through it all are the students, who much too often must turn to the SDS, which on most university campuses seems to provide the only effective leadership.

As seeds sown a decade ago in Berkeley are broadcast across the country, it becomes increasingly evident that the most devastating sustained violence has occurred either in the multiversity or at those huge bureaucratic institutions too unwieldy to be governed in traditional academic fashion. And, conversely, it has also become evident that less sprawling learning centers have managed either to avoid major upheavals or to meet disruptions with esprit and amity.

A possible solution, then, a partial one, perhaps,

211

would seem to lie in decentralization throughout the educational superstructure. I sincerely hope so.

I'm out of the academy now, and I'll probably never return. But I think it essential to keep up the attack, for the deepest personal reason—the future of my children. They've been brought up to believe in such things as honesty and kindness and truth and decency and openness and tolerance. And I want them to stay this way.

They're sensitive and exceptionally intelligent children, and someday, much too soon, they'll be ready to go off to college. But, assuming there are still colleges standing for them to go to, I may not be able to let them go. For in the academy as it has become there is no place for *good* (and as a conservative I reserve the right to use the word *good* in the most absolute, reactionary, *a priori* way) children.

And as the troubles seep down into the high schools, as the high schools become increasingly radicalized, and as the poison drips even into the lower grades, I think more and more of how nice it would be to pull out of it altogether, to remove my own children from the formal school system completely and teach them at home. Or go off to some different sort of place altogether, perhaps back to Alaska or to the Northwest Territories or to some still stable country like Australia.

The college situation seems almost hopeless. I want my children to have at least a fighting chance to retain their goodness, their decency of spirit. But the odds are against them. When they enter college, they'll still be decent children, and because they are decent, they'll have damned little chance of coming out as good as when they entered. And today when they're destroyed, they stay destroyed. In the fifties, most of the people who freaked out always kept a little something in reserve, and when the time came they rather quietly reentered society. But no longer. Today the third or fourth radical generation is coming of age and those people who were radicals in the early part of the decade are still radicals as the seventies begin. A great number of the flower children are over thirty. Jerry Rubin and Abbie Hoffman have reached middle age. But they're still children. Evil children. "We're going to get your children," they say.

And they mean it.